Going for Broke

Stolen Asset Recovery (StAR) Series

StAR—the Stolen Asset Recovery Initiative—is a partnership between the World Bank Group and the United Nations Office on Drugs and Crime (UNODC) that supports international efforts to end safe havens for corrupt funds. StAR works with developing countries and financial centers to prevent the laundering of the proceeds of corruption and to facilitate more systematic and timely return of stolen assets.

The Stolen Asset Recovery (StAR) Series supports the efforts of StAR and UNODC by providing practitioners with knowledge and policy tools that consolidate international good practice and wide-ranging practical experience on cutting-edge issues related to anti-corruption and asset recovery efforts. For more information, visit www.worldbank.org/star.

Titles in the Stolen Asset Recovery (StAR) Series

Stolen Asset Recovery: A Good Practices Guide for Non-conviction Based Asset Forfeiture (2009) by Theodore S. Greenberg, Linda M. Samuel, Wingate Grant, and Larissa Gray

Politically Exposed Persons: Preventive Measures for the Banking Sector (2010) by Theodore S. Greenberg, Larissa Gray, Delphine Schantz, Carolin Gardner, and Michael Latham

Asset Recovery Handbook: A Guide for Practitioners (2011) by Jean-Pierre Brun, Larissa Gray, Clive Scott, and Kevin Stephenson

Barriers to Asset Recovery: An Analysis of the Key Barriers and Recommendations for Action (2011) by Kevin Stephenson, Larissa Gray, and Ric Power

The Puppet Masters: How the Corrupt Use Legal Structures to Hide Stolen Assets and What to Do about It (2011) by Emile van der Does de Willebois, J. C. Sharman, Robert Harrison, Ji Won Park, and Emily Halter

Public Office, Private Interests: Accountability through Income and Asset Disclosure (2012)

On the Take: Criminalizing Illicit Enrichment to Fight Corruption (2012) by Lindy Muzila, Michelle Morales, Marianne Mathias, and Tammar Berger

Left Out of the Bargain: Settlements in Foreign Bribery Cases and Implications for Asset Recovery (2014) by Jacinta Anyango Oduor, Francisca M. U. Fernando, Agustin Flah, Dorothee Gottwald, Jeanne M. Hauch, Marianne Mathias, Ji Won Park, and Oliver Stolpe

Public Wrongs, Private Actions: Civil Lawsuits to Recover Stolen Assets (2015) by Jean-Pierre Brun, Pascale Helene Dubois, Emile van der Does de Willebois, Jeanne Hauch, Sarah Jaïs, Yannis Mekki, Anastasia Sotiropoulou, Katherine Rose Sylvester, and Mahesh Uttamchandani

Getting the Full Picture on Public Officials: A How-to Guide for Effective Financial Disclosure (2017) by Ivana M. Rossi, Laura Pop, and Tammar Berger

Going for Broke: Insolvency Tools to Support Cross-Border Asset Recovery in Corruption Cases (2020) by Jean-Pierre Brun and Molly Silver

All books in the StAR Series are available free at https://openknowledge.worldbank.org/handle/10986/2172

Going for Broke

Insolvency Tools to Support Cross-Border Asset Recovery in Corruption Cases

Jean-Pierre Brun
Molly Silver

the global voice of
the legal profession®

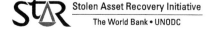

Stolen Asset Recovery Initiative
The World Bank • UNODC

ISBN (paper): 978-1-4648-1438-9
ISBN (electronic): 978-1-4648-1439-6
DOI: 10.1596/978-1-4648-1438-9
SKU: 211438

Cover photos: Bankruptcy Court Courthouse, Dayton, Ohio: © StanRohrer / iStock by Getty Images. Used with permission of StanRohrer / iStock by Getty Images. Further permission required for reuse. Magnifying glass and gavel: © designer491 / iStock by Getty Images. Used with permission of designer491 / iStock by Getty Images. Further permission required for reuse.
Cover design: Debra Naylor, Naylor Design, Washington, DC.

Library of Congress Control Number: 2019916683

Contents

Acknowledgments   *ix*
About the Authors   *xi*
Abbreviations   *xiii*
Glossary   *xv*

Introduction   1
   Objective   3
   Scope   4
   Methodology   5
   Overview of Chapters   5
   Notes   6
   References   7

1. Insolvency Proceedings and Representatives   9
   Moratorium   12
   Appointment of an Insolvency Representative   12
     The Different Authorities that May Appoint Insolvency Representatives   13
     Specific Rules and Practices for an Insolvent Bank   15
   Effects of the Appointment of an Insolvency Representative   15
   Cross-Border Recognition and Conducting Insolvency Actions Abroad   17
   Powers of Insolvency Representatives in Asset Recovery   21
     Tools Available to Collect Information and Evidence   21
     Legal Actions that Authorize Insolvency Representatives to Claim Assets   22
   Notes   25
   References   26

2. Investigative Measures Potentially Available in Insolvency
   and Civil Cases   29
   Extrajudicial Investigative Tools   29
   Discovery Databases as a Source of Information   30
   Examination of Witnesses under Standard Insolvency Practices   31
     Targets of Examination   31
     Range of Examination   33
     Use of Information   35
     Costs of Examination   36

Discovery   36
Nonstatutory Tools   36
    Anton Piller (Search and Seizure) Orders   36
    Norwich Pharmacal (Disclosure) Orders in Common Law Jurisdictions   38
    Ancillary Sealing and Gagging Orders   42
Other Investigative Tools   44
    Mareva Injunctions and Mareva by Letter in Common Law Jurisdictions   44
    Freezing Orders in Civil Law Jurisdictions   44
    Discovery in Aid of Foreign Proceedings   45
Notes   46
Reference   47

3. **Identifying Insolvency and Receivership Targets and Other Liable Persons in Corruption Cases**   49
Bribe Takers and Related Entities   49
Bribe Payers and Related Entities   52
Agents and Other Facilitators   52
Strategic and Tactical Considerations   54
    Claims against Corporate Officers, Agents, and Third-Party Facilitators   54
    The Duties of Directors and Managers of Companies   55
    Personal Liability Actions against Directors   59
    Proceedings for Fraudulent or Wrongful Trading   59
    Preferences and Transactions at Undervalue   60
    Other Breaches of Duty   61
    Derivative Actions   62
    Piercing the Corporate Veil   62
Notes   68
References   69

4. **Privilege**   71
Privilege in England   71
    Forms of Privilege at Common Law   71
    Common Interest Privilege   72
    Which Law Applies?   73
    Waiver   73
    Insolvency   73
Privilege in the United States   76
    Corporate Insolvency   76
    Personal Insolvency   76
Professional Secrecy in France   77
    Scope and Application of the Professional Secret   77
    Sanctions for Violation of Professional Secrecy by an Attorney   77
    Issues Relating to Corporate Insolvency and Bankruptcy Proceedings   77
    Issues Relating to Individual Insolvency   78
    Conclusion   78
Notes   79

5. Further Issues on the Use of Insolvency for Asset Recovery   81
  Major Challenges for Asset Recovery in Developing Jurisdictions   81
    Commencement Obstacles   81
    Unregulated or Insufficiently Regulated Insolvency Representatives   82
    Ineffective or Nonexistent Anti-Avoidance System   82
    Slow, Unresponsive, or Inexperienced Judicial Systems and Lawyers   82
  Ineffective or Nonexistent Collateral Registry Systems   83
    Impediments to Enforcement   84
    Transparency and Accountability of Legal Insolvency Frameworks   84
  Recognition and Use of Laws and Proceedings in Cross-Border Insolvency   84
    The UNCITRAL Model Law on Cross-Border Insolvency   84
    United Kingdom Cross-Border Insolvency Regulations 2006   88
  International and Institutional Considerations   89
    International Considerations   89
  The Conflict between State Confiscation of Criminal Assets and
    Insolvency Proceedings   91
  Notes   98
  References   101

**Appendix A. Country-Specific Regulations for
Insolvency Representatives**   103
  Notes   122

Appendix B. Website Resources   123
  International Organizations and Bodies   123
    World Bank Group   123
    Stolen Asset Recovery (StAR) Initiative   123
    United Nations   123
    United Nations Commission on International Trade Law   123
    Organisation for Economic Co-operation and Development
      Convention on Combating Bribery of Foreign Public Officials in
      International Business   123
  Organizations, Rating Agencies, and Bar Associations that Track
    Asset Recovery Attorneys   124
  Online Sources for Case Law   124

Boxes
I.1   Case Study on the Appointment of Insolvency Representatives   2
1.1   World Bank Principle C4.2: Commencement   9
1.2   Just and Equitable Winding Up   10
1.3   Using Insolvency Proceedings in Asset Recovery   11
1.4   World Bank Principle D7: Role of Regulatory or Supervisory Bodies   14
1.5   World Bank Principle D8: Competence and Integrity of Insolvency
       Representatives   14
1.6   Overview of the Powers of an Insolvency Representative   16

1.7   U.K. Supreme Court Rules on Cross-Border Insolvencies: The Limits of Universalism in *Rubin v. Eurofinance S.A.*   18

1.8   U.S. Court Grants Recognition of Former Russian Business Owner's Bankruptcy   20

1.9   World Bank Principle C11: Avoidable Transactions   23

2.1   *Crumpler ex rel. Global Tradewaves Ltd. v. Global Tradewaves, in re Global Tradewaves Ltd.*   33

2.2   *Clarke v. Bank of Nova Scotia Jamaica Ltd.*   41

2.3   *Marcus A. Wide v. FirstCaribbean International Bank*   43

3.1   Case Study on Just and Equitable Winding Up and the Appointment of an Insolvency Representative—*Montrow International Ltd.*   51

3.2   *Kirschner v. KPMG LLP and Teachers' Retirement System of Louisiana v. PricewaterhouseCoopers, LLP*   53

3.3   Case Study on the Principle of the "Controlling Mind"   56

3.4   World Bank Principle B2—Directors' Obligations in the Period Approaching Insolvency   58

3.5   *Prest v. Petrodel Resources Ltd.*   63

3.6   *Wood v. Baker*   64

3.7   *Bankruptcy Estate of Petroforte v. Securinvest Holdings S.A.*   65

3.8   *Bankruptcy Estate of Mabe Brasil v. Mabe/General Electric/ Penteado Family*   65

3.9   *MMX Sudeste under reorganization v. Batista*   66

5.1   World Bank Principle C15: International Considerations   89

5.2   World Bank Principle D1: Implementation—Institutional and Regulatory Frameworks   90

5.3   World Bank Principles and Best Practices   90

5.4   The Stanford International Bank (in Liquidation)   92

5.5   SK Foods LP   95

5.6   Banco Santos   97

Acknowledgments

Going for Broke: Insolvency Tools to Support Cross-Border Asset Recovery in Corruption Cases is published by the World Bank–United Nations Office on Drugs and Crime (UNODC) Stolen Asset Recovery Initiative (StAR) in collaboration with the Asset Recovery Committee of the Legal Practice Division of the International Bar Association and is produced by kind permission of the International Bar Association, London, United Kingdom.

The handbook was written and coordinated by Jean-Pierre Brun (Financial Integrity Unit), Molly Silver (Financial Integrity Unit), and practitioners from around the world. Yves Klein, Edward Davis, Martin Kenney, Elizabeth O'Brian, Lynne Gregory, Annette Escobar, Stephane Bonifassi, Victoire Chatelin, Rodrigo Kaysserlian, and Andres Federico Martinez each contributed to the drafting of the handbook's chapters. Their time and expertise were invaluable in developing a practical tool to assist policy makers and practitioners interested in using insolvency tools to recover the proceeds of corruption.

The authors are especially grateful to Emile J. Van der Does de Willebois (Coordinator, StAR), Mahesh Uttamchandani (Practice Manager, FCI-EFI), and Alfonso Garcia Mora (Global Director, FCI-EFI) for their ongoing support and guidance.

The team benefited from many insightful comments during the peer review process, which was chaired by Yira Mascaro (Practice Manager, FCI-EFI). The peer reviewers were Anthony Fariello (Lead Counsel, World Bank), Fernando Dancausa (Senior Financial Sector Specialist, EFNFI), David Burdette (INSOL International), and James Maton (Cooley LLP).

The handbook also benefited from the guidance and contributions of Stephen Baker (Baker & Partners, Chairman of the International Bar Association Asset Recovery Subcommittee), Christopher Redmond (Redmond Law Firm), and Felicity Toube (South Square).

A special thanks to Keesook Viehweg (Program Assistant, FCI-EFI) for administrative support and Sara Balagh (Georgetown University Law Center) for assistance in editing the handbook.

About the Authors

Jean-Pierre Brun is a senior financial specialist at the World Bank. He worked as a prosecutor and investigative judge in France and as a director of forensic and fraud investigations at Deloitte Finance in Paris. In 2008, he joined the World Bank, where he works on anti–money laundering, terrorist financing, illicit financial flows, and stolen asset recovery, providing technical assistance and training to investigators, prosecutors, and judges dealing with financial crime. He is the lead author of various publications, including *Asset Recovery Handbook: A Guide for Practitioners*, *Public Wrongs–Private Actions: Civil Lawsuits to Recover Stolen Assets*, and *Identification and Quantification of the Proceeds of Corruption*.

Molly Silver is a consultant in the Finance, Competitiveness, and Innovation Group at the World Bank. She previously served as a presidential management fellow in the departments of Treasury and Defense. She then worked on international policy strategy at technology companies, including Facebook, Inc., and Palantir Technologies. Molly studied political science as an undergraduate at New York University and American foreign policy as a graduate student at the Johns Hopkins School of Advanced International Studies.

Abbreviations

COMI	center of main interest
DOJ	Department of Justice
EBRD	European Bank for Reconstruction and Development
ECHR	European Convention on Human Rights
EU	European Union
FBI	Federal Bureau of Investigation
FCPA	Foreign Corrupt Practices Act
FIU	Financial Intelligence Unit
GDP	gross domestic product
GE	General Electric
IOH	insolvency office holder
MLAT	mutual legal assistance treaty
PEP	politically exposed person
PILA	private international law act
SEC	Securities and Exchange Commission
StAR	Stolen Asset Recovery Initiative
UNCAC	United Nations Convention against Corruption
UNCITRAL	United Nations Commission on International Trade Law

All monetary amounts are in U.S. dollars unless otherwise indicated.

Glossary

Administrator: A representative who has been charged with rescuing a business, rather than closing it, unless the context requires otherwise.

Arbitration: A procedure under which parties agree to resolve a dispute by submitting it to one or more private persons who have no financial interest in the outcome. Arbitration clauses can be found in international contracts and bilateral investment treaties.

Assets: Assets of every kind, whether corporeal or incorporeal, movable or immovable, tangible or intangible, and legal documents or instruments evidencing title to or an interest in such assets (United Nations 2005, art. 2(e)). The term is used interchangeably with "property."

Avoidance actions: The cancellation of transactions that took place during a period before the insolvency of an enterprise. Such transactions can be, for example, fraudulent, gratuitous, preferential, or outside the ordinary course of business.

Bankruptcy: The legal procedure for managing the insolvency of individuals and businesses.

Beneficial owner: The true owner of securities or property who is rightfully entitled to their benefits; the beneficial owner is often different from the title holder, which may be a financial institution holding securities on behalf of clients.

Bona fide purchaser: A third party with an interest in an asset subject to confiscation who did not know of the conduct giving rise to the confiscation or who, on learning of the conduct giving rise to confiscation, did all that reasonably could be expected under the circumstances to terminate the use of the asset. The term is used interchangeably with "innocent owner."

Bribery: Any of the promising, offering, or giving of an undue advantage to a national, international, or foreign public official and the acceptance of an undue advantage by such an official.

Civil action: A noncriminal action brought to enforce, redress, or protect a private or civil right. An action brought by a private person is a private action; an action brought by a government is a public action. The term is used interchangeably with "lawsuit."

Civil forfeiture: The seizure by a government of property upon suspicion of its involvement in illegal activity.

Claimant: A party asserting an interest in an asset, including a third party, innocent owner, defendant, target, or offender. The term is used interchangeably with "plaintiff."

Collateral security: Security given in addition to a senior security, and subordinate to it, intended to guaranty its validity or convertibility or ensure its performance; if the senior security fails, the creditor may recover through recourse to the collateral security.

Compensation: The amount of money that places the victim in the financial position it would have held absent the corruption.

Confiscation: The permanent deprivation of assets by order of a court or other competent authority. The term is used interchangeably with "civil forfeiture." Persons or entities that hold an interest in the funds or other assets at the time of the confiscation lose all rights to those funds or assets.

Contempt of court: Any willful disobedience or disregard of a court order that interferes with a judge's ability to administer justice.

Contract: A covenant or agreement between two or more persons, with lawful consideration or cause, to do, or abstain from doing, some act.

Corruption: The act of an official or fiduciary who unlawfully and wrongfully uses his station or character to procure some benefit for himself or for another person, contrary to duty and the rights of others.

Damages: Pecuniary compensation that may be recovered by a plaintiff for loss, injury, or harm caused by a breach of duty, including criminal wrongdoing or immoral conduct. Compensatory damages refer to the monetary harm to the economic position of the person who has suffered the damage. The loss of profits represents the profit that could reasonably have been expected but that was forfeited because of the vitiated contract or the breach.

Defendant: Any party who is required to answer the complaint of a plaintiff in a civil lawsuit before a court, or any party who has been formally charged or accused of violating a criminal statute.

Derivative action or suit: A lawsuit on behalf of a corporation by its shareholders against a director or officer for damages for failure of duty or mismanagement.

Embezzlement: Fraudulent appropriation to his own use or benefit by a clerk, agent, trustee, public officer, or other person acting in a fiduciary capacity of public funds or property entrusted to him by another.

Enforcement (civil judgment): The collection of the value stipulated in a judgment against an asset held by a defendant.

Estate: An interest in land or any other property.

Forum: A court of justice or judicial tribunal; a place of jurisdiction; a place where a remedy is sought; a place of litigation.

Frozen asset: An asset that cannot be sold or used as legal leverage owing to a legal ruling. The asset cannot be sold or used for security until the ruling is satisfied or reversed.

Gag order: An order of a court that restricts the dissemination of information about a pending case.

In personam: Latin for "directed toward a particular person." In a confiscation or lawsuit, a legal action against a specific person.

In rem: Latin for "against a thing." In a confiscation or lawsuit, a legal action against a specific asset.

Insolvency: The conditions that support proceedings in court (including liquidation and reorganization) and out of court (including receivership) to conduct the winding up of a company that is bankrupt or was created for fraudulent purposes.

International asset recovery: The process by which the proceeds of corruption transferred abroad are recovered and repatriated to the country from which they were taken or to their rightful owners.

Lawsuit: A private action between two persons in a court of law in which a plaintiff who claims to have incurred loss as a result of a defendant's actions seeks a legal or equitable remedy. The term is used interchangeably with "civil action."

Liquidation: The sale of a debtor's assets, the proceeds of which are used for the benefit of creditors.

Money laundering: The act of taking money obtained illegally and investing it to make it appear as if it was obtained legally.

Mutual legal assistance treaty: The process by which jurisdictions seek and provide assistance in gathering information, intelligence, and evidence for investigations; in implementing provisional measures; and in enforcing foreign orders and judgments.

Personal claim: A claim against a person. A plaintiff who has suffered economic damages can demand to be paid or compensated from the assets of the person who caused the damage.

Prima facie: Legal term meaning that a proposition or claim is accepted as correct until proven otherwise.

Proceeds of crime: Any asset derived from or obtained, directly or indirectly, through the commission of an offense. In most jurisdictions, commingled assets are included.

Proprietary claim: A claim by the beneficial owner of a piece of property or an asset asking the court to return the item or its equivalent value.

Provisional measure: The temporary prohibition against the transfer, conversion, disposition, or movement of assets or temporary assumption of custody or control of assets pursuant to an order of a court or other competent authority. The term is used interchangeably with "freezing (of an asset)," "restraint," and "seizure."

Receivership: The process through which all property subject to claims is placed under the control of an independent receiver, who operates the company or manages its assets in event of a receivership. Some contracts between borrowers and creditors authorize the appointment of a receiver if a secured creditor is not being paid or if a lender finds the company's management practices dubious. Court action is not required.

Recognition (civil judgment): The acceptance by one court of the conclusion of another court without hearing evidence or engaging in an independent decision-making process. The second court issues its own judgment stating substantially the same conclusion.

Reorganization: The restructuring of the debt obligations of a bankrupt or insolvent company. During reorganization, the debtor retains ownership of its assets and continues business operations. The debtor renegotiates the terms of its debt obligations to creditors.

Restitution: A court order directing the (1) return of an item to its legal owner, (2) restoration of damaged property to its original state, or (3) payment of compensation to a victim.

Restraining order: A mandatory injunction issued by a judge or a court that restrains any person from using or disposing of the assets named in the order, pending the outcome of confiscation proceedings. Court authorization is generally required, but some jurisdictions permit restraining orders to be issued by prosecutors or other law enforcement authorities.

Seizure: Taking physical possession of a targeted asset. Court orders are generally required, but in some jurisdictions law enforcement agencies are entitled to seize assets.

Tort: A civil wrong, giving rise to a claim for damages.

Tracing: The process by which a claimant demonstrates the disposition of his property, identifies its proceeds, and justifies his claim that the proceeds can properly be regarded as representing his property.

Unjust enrichment: The principle according to which a person should not be permitted to unfairly enrich himself at the expense of another, but should be required to make restitution for property or benefits unjustly received.

Winding up: The process of settling the accounts and liquidating the assets of a partnership or company, for the purpose of making a distribution and dissolving the concern.

Witness: Someone who, either voluntarily or under compulsion, provides testimonial evidence, either oral or written, of what he or she knows or claims to know about the matter before a court or before an official authorized to take such testimony. Evidence provided by witnesses, including expert witnesses, is frequently important in both civil and criminal asset recovery cases.

In her opening statement to the 22nd session of the Human Rights Council in March 2013, Navi Pillay, High Commissioner for Human Rights, stated:

> Let us be clear. Corruption kills. The money stolen through corruption every year is enough to feed the world's hungry 80 times over. Nearly 870 million people go to bed hungry every night, many of them children; corruption denies them their right to food, and, in some cases, their right to life. Bribes and theft swell the total cost of projects to provide safe drinking water and sanitation around the world by as much as 40 percent.[1]

Corruption is the abuse of entrusted power for private gain. It hurts everyone whose life, livelihood, and happiness depend on the integrity of people in a position of authority. Corruption holds back economic development, prevents a free market from operating for businesses and consumers, and further exploits already marginalized groups. In the words of leading anticorruption expert Richard Cassin, "[vulnerable] people—hated because they look or sound different, worship another God, or once came from somewhere else—rely on the rule of law for their safety and survival. When the rule of law is replaced by graft, the outcome for the weakest among us is too often catastrophic."[2]

Economist Daniel Kaufmann has estimated that 2 percent of global GDP is lost to bribery alone every year. But these corrupt proceeds may not be gone forever—nations can use asset recovery to fight corruption, restoring stolen funds to the people for sustainable development and deterring further corruption. Because assets stolen in corruption schemes are often moved to different jurisdictions, recovery efforts demand international cooperation. The international framework governing such cooperation is laid down in the 2003 United Nations Convention Against Corruption (UNCAC), which went into force in 2005. The first article of the extensive chapter on asset recovery declares the return of assets "a fundamental principle of the convention" and obligates states that are party to the convention to "afford one another the widest measure of cooperation" (United Nations 2004).

Despite the great advances in international efforts to recover assets from corrupt officials since the UNCAC went into effect, there is still much work to do. Governments often use criminal prosecution and confiscation, as well as civil lawsuits. However, barriers to successful asset recovery are numerous. They include the lack of political will to investigate and charge corrupt politicians; a dearth of capacity, expertise, and resources to pursue cases or cooperate internationally; and the existence of a global financial system that enables corrupt officials to rapidly move and conceal illicit funds.[3]

These challenges can impede justice in many corruption cases. This book offers a rarely used way to recover the proceeds of corruption—insolvency proceedings—thus contributing to the development of an additional tool for the realization of the UNCAC's principle on asset recovery.

As described in the case study in box I.1, victims of corruption may be able to use insolvency processes to gain control of assets held by or on behalf of debtors. The process typically follows a standard pattern, although it may vary by jurisdiction. An insolvency representative is appointed to take control of the debtor and its assets and can ask the debtor's depository bank for information on the debtor's bank accounts and the debtor's

---

BOX I.1   Case Study on the Appointment of Insolvency Representatives

Federal Republic of Brazil and Municipality of São Paulo v. Durant International Ltd. and Kildare Finance Ltd.[a]

Paulo Maluf, the former mayor of São Paulo, was convicted of committing fraud against the taxpayers of Brazil and São Paolo. Authorities found that he stole approximately 20 percent of the funds that were intended for the construction of a highway around the city. While in office, he ordered the head contractor on the highway project to inflate invoices, which enabled him to siphon funds without causing alarm. Other false invoices were issued by subcontractors, many of whom did no work. A large amount of cash was generated, laundered through *dolleiros* (unlicensed money brokers), and then deposited into bank accounts in several U.S. states. From there, the proceeds were transferred to a bank account in New York, and some were transferred to Jersey, where they were held in a complicated trust as well as in two private companies—Durant International Ltd. (Durant) and Kildare Finance Ltd. (Kildare). Some of the funds remained in bank accounts in Jersey, but the bulk was invested through unit trusts in shares in a publicly traded company in Brazil.

Durant and Kildare were incorporated in the British Virgin Islands. After uncovering the scheme, the governments of Brazil and São Paulo sued Durant and Kildare for their involvement in the fraud. They alleged that Durant and Kildare knowingly received the proceeds of a public corruption scheme and dishonestly assisted in the fraud. Brazil and São Paulo won, and the Jersey court ordered Durant and Kildare to pay $30 million to Brazil and São Paulo. The plaintiffs recovered $2.1 million from bank accounts in Jersey.

Brazil and São Paulo were still owed substantial amounts by Durant and Kildare, both of which refused to pay the Jersey judgment. Brazil and São Paulo used a statutory demand for creditor's rights in bankruptcy, an insolvency tool, to recover what was still owed to them. They applied to the British Virgin Islands court for insolvency representatives to be appointed over Durant and Kildare. The British Virgin Islands court agreed and appointed two partners of a large accounting firm as insolvency representatives. The insolvency representatives were recognized in the Jersey court and took control of the trust structure. They have wide powers to demand access to records and to interview witnesses. Because Durant and Kildare have been declared insolvent, the insolvency representatives retain control of the companies and all the powers its directors and officers previously held, as a matter of law.

a. [2015] UKPC 35.

---

counsel and accountant for files and records. (Once appointed, the insolvency representative is entitled to that information; attorney-client privilege no longer applies.) The insolvency representative can fire and terminate employees—the board of directors, the chairman of the board, the president, the treasurer, and the secretary no longer have any authority. The insolvency representative has standing to bring actions to recover preferences and to recover fraudulent conveyances.

The terms "bankruptcy" and "insolvency" have different definitions in different legal systems and are sometimes used interchangeably. In this publication, insolvency is used more broadly as the overarching term to describe court proceedings that include liquidation and reorganization and out-of-court proceedings such as receivership. The term insolvency also refers to bankruptcy unless another meaning is indicated; for example, bankruptcy would be used to refer to the insolvency of an individual as opposed to a corporation. The terms "receiver" and "receivership" refer to the process of taking control of assets or businesses for the benefit of a particular creditor as opposed to a body of creditors; a process designed to preserve assets; or the status of a business pending the resolution of a particular proceeding or the occurrence of a specified event. The term "administrator" refers to a representative who has been charged with rescuing a business, rather than closing it, unless the context otherwise requires.

In this book, the term "insolvency representative" refers to the person fulfilling the range of functions that may be performed in any kind of insolvency proceeding, irrespective of his or her specific goal (liquidation or reorganization). Insolvency representatives may, under local law, be called "administrators," "trustees," "supervisors," "receivers," "curators," "official" or "judicial" managers, or "commissioners." See UNCITRAL (2004, 174) and Flores and Inacio (2016). Insolvency proceedings typically require the replacement, in whole or in part, of the debtor's management authority. Upon appointment, the insolvency representative has absolute control over the business affairs of the debtor and the debtor's assets (EBRD 2014).

Objective

This guidebook is intended to inform policy makers, public officials, and those who have been entrusted with recovering their nations' stolen assets how insolvency can be used to pursue proceeds of corruption. It may also serve as a quick reference for other practitioners—insolvency professionals, auditors, financial institutions, in-house counsel, and others who deal with corruption.

Although there is no guarantee of success, the use of insolvency in asset recovery provides numerous benefits not readily available in other recovery frameworks. As with any asset recovery effort, however, there are hurdles and challenges.

The insolvency mechanisms described in this book can be used against both bribe takers and bribe payers. Many legal systems have comparable provisions in place, such as the ability to petition for the bankruptcy of an individual, the insolvency of a corporation, and the reversal or voiding of past transactions within a specified time after the initiation of insolvency procedures. Although not all jurisdictions offer equivalent procedures, an in-depth analysis of all jurisdictions is beyond the scope of this publication.[4] The authors speak of insolvency and bankruptcy in general, giving examples of significant differences among jurisdictions when relevant.

Scope

This publication focuses on insolvency as an additional civil remedy for the asset recovery practitioner in large corruption investigations and proceedings. The recovery of proceeds of corruption is often sought through criminal prosecution and confiscation or civil lawsuits. Under appropriate circumstances, an insolvency proceeding can also be an effective mechanism, albeit one with advantages and disadvantages. Insolvency is most likely to be beneficial when bribes and stolen funds have been routed through a special-purpose vehicle for concealment and laundering. Although reference may be made to other civil remedies and theories of recovery when appropriate, this guidebook does not address noninsolvency civil remedies or actions.

This guidebook addresses insolvency-related investigations and litigation for asset recovery stemming from official corruption. We focus in particular on common law systems, such as the United Kingdom, the United States, and many offshore common law jurisdictions, which offer the clearest path for asset recovery through insolvency proceedings. We also refer to civil law systems, such as those in France and Switzerland, whose legal systems often deal with illicit financial flows.

Several offshore jurisdictions are relevant in international insolvency cases and feature prominently in this book. Companies in the British Virgin Islands are frequently used in offshore structures, as are those in other offshore jurisdictions that specialize in corporate formation, such as Bermuda, the Cayman Islands, the Isle of Man, and Panama. Crown Dependencies, including Guernsey and Jersey, which specialize in trusts, feature in the discussion of trustees. The court system of the British Virgin Islands in particular has robust protections for those who have been the victims of fraud and corruption. Similarly, the courts in Jersey also offer protection to victims of fraud through the misuse of financial services. Significant expertise has emerged in Jersey and the British Virgin Islands on these matters, and we highlight several cases that demonstrate the progress made.

This publication should provide the reader with a solid understanding of how insolvency procedures can effectively be employed to either complement an existing asset recovery action, whether civil or criminal, or act as a stand-alone procedure for recovery. The guidebook is not designed to be a detailed compendium of law and practices and should be read by practitioners in tandem with the rules of their jurisdiction. The authors hope that practitioners in any jurisdiction affected by corruption will find useful references and ideas for their areas of practice.

Methodology

This publication identifies potential methods of asset recovery in insolvency proceedings. Although the book incorporates examples of legislation, concepts, and practices that are relevant for both civil law and common law jurisdictions, as well as developed or emerging countries, some jurisdictions (including the United Kingdom and some other common law jurisdictions) feature the world's most developed institutional insolvency systems, including highly skilled judges and insolvency practitioners.

Although tools that have been successfully applied in the United Kingdom and other common law jurisdictions are not necessarily applicable in other legal systems, most jurisdictions, including civil law jurisdictions, have equivalent concepts or concepts that enable comparable results. These tools are described as comprehensively as possible for the use of jurisdictions establishing legislation or implementing their own systems.

In addition, applying the tools in some jurisdictions may be challenging. This publication does not recommend legal reforms or mandate implementation of specific tools, but highlights potential strategies or practices that may be similar to those allowed in other legal systems or in other cases of asset recovery. The publication also recognizes that the main purpose of insolvency proceedings is to preserve the interests protected by insolvency legislation (including, but not limited to, creditors' interests). Using the powers of insolvency representatives or other relevant practitioners to identify, trace, and recover proceeds of corruption does not imply that these practitioners should be regarded as enforcing criminal law.

Overview of Chapters

Chapter 1 describes the role of insolvency representatives in formal insolvency processes, under which they can be appointed by commercial courts and judges to administer or liquidate the estate of a natural or legal person whose liabilities exceed his or its assets. The appointment of an insolvency representative typically triggers a moratorium on any further transfer of assets. If a bankrupt entity has assets within the jurisdiction in which it was declared bankrupt, the insolvency process will prevent any further dissipation of the bankrupt estate. Chapter 1 details the effect of such a moratorium internationally, as well as the investigatory powers of the representative.

Chapter 2 outlines the investigative measures that can be used in insolvency procedures. This chapter examines the tools, both statutory and nonstatutory, available to insolvency representatives, including powers of examination of individuals, discovery or delivery of documents, and orders for the provision of specified information. The chapter also discusses ancillary relief designed to maintain the integrity of an investigation, such as seal and gag orders, as well as the powers of courts to dispense with requirements to give notice to parties and to hear matters without notice and in camera.

Chapter 3 discusses how to recover assets from bribe takers through insolvency proceedings. Although the focus is typically on bribe payers, agents and facilitators, who are often used as intermediaries to solicit and pay bribes, can also be targeted through the insolvency process. The chapter examines the various causes of action against parties, both criminal and civil, explaining the difference between those causes of action that accrue prior to the insolvency and those that accrue after. The chapter details the options available to insolvency representatives, including taking over the conduct of existing proceedings, commencing proceedings on behalf of the estate, and assignment of causes of action in exchange for value. Derivative actions are also explained and discussed, as are issues concerning the legal standing of insolvency representatives to bring particular types of actions. Finally, the chapter examines the notion of piercing the corporate veil.

Chapter 4 explains the implications of legal privilege in insolvency proceedings in the United Kingdom, the United States, and France. The rules on legal professional privilege can impair the insolvency representative's ability to obtain or use information. Common law jurisdictions have historically recognized privilege as a fundamental principle of justice and grant wide-ranging protection against the disclosure of both lawyer-client communications and, when litigation is contemplated, a wider class of documents with third parties.

Chapter 5 deals with additional issues in the use of insolvency proceedings for asset recovery, including critical differences between developed and developing jurisdictions and cross-border issues that may arise when corrupt assets or defendants are located in other jurisdictions. Legal frameworks are available to ensure the enforcement of insolvency legislation or orders made by the jurisdiction of the insolvency proceeding and the resolution of insolvencies that involve two or more jurisdictions. This chapter also explains how to address the conflict between state confiscation of criminal assets and the recovery of funds through insolvency proceedings and proposes tactics for dealing with the delays that arise in criminal proceedings.

Notes

1. Opening Statement by Navi Pillay, High Commissioner for Human Rights. Panel on "The Negative Impact of Corruption on Human Rights" (March 27, 2013), www .ohchr.org/Documents/Issues/Development/GoodGovernance/Corruption /HRCaseAgainstCorruption.pdf.
2. Richard L. Cassin, "Rampant Graft and the Risk of Atrocities: Are Whistleblower Reward Programs Really a Good Idea?" *The FCPA Blog* (May 15, 2014) (accessed December 26, 2018). http://www.fcpablog.com/blog/2014/5/15/rampant-graft-and -the-risk-of-atrocities.html.
3. For a detailed discussion of the types of problems encountered in international asset recovery, see Brun et al. (2011).
4. See appendix A for jurisdiction-specific analyses of a selection of relevant procedures and regulations.

References

Brun, Jean-Pierre, Gabriele Dunker, Larissa Alanna Gray, Melissa Panjer, Richard John Power, and Kevin Mark Stephenson. 2011. *Barriers to Asset Recovery*. Washington, DC: World Bank.

EBRD (European Bank for Reconstruction and Development). 2014. *Assessment of Insolvency Office Holders: Review of the Profession in the EBRD Region*. London: EBRD.

Flores, Marta, and Emmanuelle Inacio. 2016. "Report on the Regulation of Insolvency Office Holders," Insolvency Office Holders Forum, INSOL Europe, May 4.

IMF (International Monetary Fund). 2016. "Corruption: Costs and Mitigating Strategies." IMF Staff Discussion Note No. 16/05, IMF, Washington, DC.

UNCITRAL (United Nations Commission on International Trade Law). 2004. *Legislative Guide on Insolvency Law*. Vienna: UNCITRAL.

United Nations. 2004. *United Nations Convention Against Corruption*. Vienna: United Nations Office on Drugs and Crime.

1. Insolvency Proceedings and Representatives

The ability to commence an insolvency proceeding is crucial for asset recovery. Typically, there are two standard tests for commencement of insolvency proceedings: (1) illiquidity, or the inability to pay existing obligations as they become due in the ordinary course of business; and (2) the balance sheet test, when liabilities exceed assets. Countries will generally use one or both tests. These two tests are discussed in World Bank Principle C4.2 (box 1.1), one of the World Bank's Principles for Effective Insolvency and Creditor/Debtor Rights Systems, which set out a range of benchmarks, based on international best practices, for evaluating the effectiveness of domestic insolvency systems.

The traditional commencement tests, while internationally recognized as best practices for opening a standard insolvency case, may be insufficient to recover stolen assets through insolvency proceedings. This guidebook discusses a third method of commencement, just and equitable grounds (see chapter 3 for more details). Some jurisdictions addressed in this book, such as the British Virgin Islands, the Cayman Islands, and the United Kingdom,[1] permit a declaration of insolvency on just and equitable grounds when business has been conducted illegally.[2]

Winding up a company is a legal tool (see box 1.2). Should an insolvency framework not provide just and equitable grounds for winding up, the enterprise will have to meet one of the standard tests for commencement of insolvency proceedings before any action can be taken. Although insolvency is not generally relevant in corruption cases, insolvency representatives can play a key role in the subsequent asset recovery process, even when their primary role is to protect the interests of creditors and other parties. They have a duty to report to criminal agencies and supporting institutions any illegal or irregular conduct uncovered in the administration of an estate and thus can aid the

---

BOX 1.1   World Bank Principle C4.2: Commencement

Commencement criteria and presumptions about insolvency should be clearly defined in the law. The preferred test to commence an insolvency proceeding should be the debtor's inability to pay debts as they mature, although insolvency may also exist where the debtor's liabilities exceed the value of its assets, provided that the values of assets and liabilities are measured on the basis of fair-market values.

A court may order the winding up of a company, even if the company is not technically bankrupt or insolvent, if the court believes that there are just and equitable grounds for doing so—a decision that is largely at the discretion of the court. Reasons for ordering the just and equitable winding up of a company have varied from country to country. They can include deadlock within a company's management, loss of substratum (the loss of the reason for a company to exist), or abuse of power by a company's leadership (often by the suppression of minority owners). This type of ruling has been used to wind up companies that were created for fraudulent purposes.

detection and identification of illicit assets. In cases of embezzlement of public funds, the main creditor of an estate is the government; therefore, insolvency representatives should coordinate with the investigative authorities to recover illicit assets. In other circumstances, companies may be created, either domestically or overseas, for the sole purpose of holding illicit assets stolen from the government or purchased with the proceeds of corruption. Insolvency representatives can use their powers to recover proceeds of corruption in two ways:

- The insolvency representative acts as the representative of an insolvent person or entity that was deprived of assets following corrupt activities conducted by one of its directors or managers, that is, the insolvent entity is the victim.
- The insolvency representative acts on behalf of the person or entity that perpetrated or assisted in the corruption.

For example, an investigation may demonstrate that a company's only activity was to issue fictitious invoices to justify the transfer of funds used to pay bribes to directors or managers of another company. Other cases involve the use of companies to transfer or manage assets purchased with proceeds of corruption. Companies that are used as instruments of corruption or for the laundering of illicit proceeds can be targeted as insolvent companies or on just and equitable grounds, when available. If prosecutors or victims of corruption demonstrate that these companies do not have sufficient assets to cover their liabilities or claim not to have assets, hide assets, or simply refuse to pay what is owed, the claimant can ask the court to appoint an insolvency representative who will use his investigative and legal powers to identify information or assets that are essential to the recovery process.

For a government seeking to recover proceeds of corruption that a former official invested, managed, or laundered through businesses or companies, insolvency can be a productive strategic step, especially if the government can show that the entity is liable for unpaid taxes, or when, as is the case in some civil law countries, the insolvency legislation allows prosecutors to petition courts to open a bankruptcy case. Not all countries have insolvency regulations that allow prosecutors to do so.[3]

As shown in box 1.3, when a person or an entity effectively defaults, a creditor can apply to a court or another competent authority and request that the person or entity be declared insolvent. In insolvency proceedings, the first step is usually a moratorium, or freeze, on all transactions, followed by the appointment of an insolvency representative to manage the assets and ensure that they are used fairly to reimburse creditors. In corruption cases that are pursued through insolvency proceedings, the appointment of an insolvency representative is a crucial step.

The purpose of insolvency proceedings for asset recovery is to seize and sell assets of the debtor-defendant and distribute the money equitably to creditors and other injured parties, thereby protecting their rights. Proceedings are generally conducted, monitored, or decided in court, through liquidation or reorganization, in similar out-of-court proceedings.

The appointment of an insolvency representative and, more generally, the launch of insolvency proceedings have an immediate legal effect on the asset recovery process.

BOX 1.3   Using Insolvency Proceedings in Asset Recovery

In this hypothetical example, a Latin American country has been the victim of substantial theft by corruption. A government official in the country entered into a series of contracts on behalf of a state-owned bus service provider with bus manufacturing companies in France, Germany, Italy, and the United Kingdom. The contractual sums due were paid by the state-owned bus service provider into bank accounts held by the bus manufacturers in each of the four European countries.

Shortly before each of the contracts was signed, offshore companies owned by the bus manufacturers entered into contracts for consulting services with four Isle of Man companies. The Isle of Man companies billed the manufacturers for substantial sums, which were paid from bank accounts, held in the names of subsidiaries of the bus manufacturers, in Singapore. The funds were then transferred into a variety of complex investment holdings. Anticorruption officers in the Latin American country learned of the scheme and successfully sued three of the consultants in the Isle of Man.

Because there were evidentiary issues with the case against the fourth consultant, it was not included in the initial legal proceeding. However, the judgment in the other three cases was so heavily in favor of the claimant that anticorruption officers decided to evaluate other options to pursue a case against the fourth consultant. All four consultants were part of a scheme to defraud the Latin American country. The companies had no commercial rationale. Representatives of the Latin American government, attempting to recover the stolen assets, petitioned for the fourth consultant to be wound up on just and equitable grounds because it existed only for demonstrably fraudulent purposes. The Isle of Man court ordered that the company be wound up, and an insolvency representative was appointed. The assets held by the company were recovered and repaid to the Latin American country.

Cross-border effects may allow the representative to seek the identification and recovery of the bankrupt entity's assets in foreign jurisdictions. Finally, insolvency representatives have two types of power that are relevant and crucial for the asset recovery process: investigatory powers and legal powers to claim assets.

The elements of insolvency proceedings are addressed in the remaining sections of chapter 1.

Moratorium

Moratorium refers to the suspension of activity, especially the suspension of collection of debts by a private business, government, or under a court order. In insolvency law, it means a halt to the right to collect a debt from the insolvent company as soon as the insolvency proceedings have commenced.

Appointment of an Insolvency Representative

The insolvency representative's main role is to maximize the interests of creditors and other parties harmed by the insolvency or the fraudulent activity. Policy makers and practitioners should keep in mind that the powers of insolvency representatives in terminal insolvency proceedings, which wind up a business, may differ from those in rescue proceedings, which reorganize a business. In the United Kingdom, for example, the representative will have powers under a rescue proceeding similar to those available for vulnerable transactions and powers of examination.

To retrieve stolen assets, the insolvency representative will be required to identify and retrieve the illegally obtained proceeds stolen by bribe takers or others committing fraud. Although insolvency laws have much in common across jurisdictions, the position of insolvency representative varies considerably between jurisdictions.[4]

Insolvency representatives generally have the benefit of broad powers to access information and to demand testimony from individuals such as directors or managers. The availability of a statutory mandate to investigate, often under the protection of secrecy, has proven to be a powerful weapon in large asset recovery cases. The declaration of insolvency and the ensuing appointment of an insolvency representative has the automatic effect of freezing the status quo and empowering the insolvency representative to act on behalf of the bankrupt entity. Among other things, an insolvency representative is generally entitled to bring claims against a company's former directors for their wrongdoing in involving the company in a corruption scheme. Claims for restitution or damages can also be made against third parties dishonestly assisting with or participating in that wrongdoing. If defendants or assets are located in a foreign jurisdiction, the powers of an insolvency representative may be more easily enforced abroad than those of a creditor.

Insolvency representatives can also be appointed to take control of and manage a debtor's assets as either a general receiver or a special receiver. A general receiver is analogous to an insolvency representative: upon appointment, the general receiver takes control of all assets and operates the businesses of the debtor until either sale or liquidation. In a special or limited receivership, the receiver takes possession only of designated assets or businesses of the debtor.

Liquidation, compulsory proceedings to sell and dispose of assets for distribution to creditors, might result from a creditor's petition to a court seeking the winding up of the company. The creditor will likely prevail if the company is unable to pay its debts. In liquidation, the insolvency representative conducts all proceedings, including the sale of remaining assets.

Jurisdictions differ as to the authorities that have the power to select and appoint insolvency representatives; these differences may depend on the type of insolvency proceeding (World Bank Principle C17 2016; UNCITRAL 2004, 176; EBRD 2014, 55).

The Different Authorities that May Appoint Insolvency Representatives

In general, there is a public model and a private-professional model for insolvency representatives. In developed jurisdictions, a professional from an international accounting firm is commonly appointed as an insolvency representative. In the public model (more common in low- and middle-income countries), an employee of the state is appointed as the insolvency representative.[5] Some jurisdictions also allow legal professionals to serve as insolvency representatives.

In most jurisdictions, depending on the type and the purpose of the insolvency proceeding, insolvency representatives are appointed by: (1) the court; (2) the court with creditor input or at the direction of the creditors; or (3) independent appointing authorities (EBRD 2014, 55). Some jurisdictions use an electronic random selection system to select and appoint representatives.

In some jurisdictions, creditors play a role in recommending and selecting the insolvency representative, provided that the person recommended meets the qualifications for serving in the specific case. In other jurisdictions, insolvency representatives are designated by the company or its directors or, in other cases, by the court at the request of a creditor. In some jurisdictions a government to which taxes are owed may have a say in the selection of the insolvency representative.

Using an independent appointing authority to select the insolvency representative has the advantage of enabling the choice of professionals with the expertise and knowledge to handle a specific case (EBRD 2014, 55). This can be particularly useful when dealing with banks, as discussed in the following section.

One or more of these approaches may be available to victims of political corruption, including the government, or other persons harmed by corruption. Which approach is correct will depend upon the facts of the case and the jurisdiction in which the debtor and the assets are located.

Although less visible, the supervision and disciplinary control of insolvency representatives is also important, and it varies considerably from jurisdiction to jurisdiction. The World Bank Principles recommend an independent system to oversee the profession, establish who is competent to act as a representative, and provide standards of conduct. Boxes 1.4 and 1.5 set out World Bank Principles D7 and D8, which identify key best practices for insolvency representative regulation.

BOX 1.4   **World Bank Principle D7: Role of Regulatory or Supervisory Bodies**

The bodies responsible for regulating or supervising insolvency representatives should:

- Be independent.

- Set standards that reflect public expectations of fairness, impartiality, transparency, and accountability.

- Have appropriate powers and resources to enable them to discharge their functions, duties, and responsibilities effectively.

In addition to the World Bank Principles, the EBRD Insolvency Office Holder (IOH) Principles set out 12 more detailed principles, including those for the qualification, remuneration, and supervision, as well as a code of ethics, for insolvency representatives. Officials establishing or reforming an insolvency representative regulatory regime should take these IOH Principles into account. These principles would also enable interested parties (such as governments, commercial banks, and law firms) to analyze the regulatory environment in the country from which they are seeking asset recovery to understand any weaknesses in the system regulating insolvency representatives.

Source: EBRD 2007.

BOX 1.5   **World Bank Principle D8: Competence and Integrity of Insolvency Representatives**

The system should ensure that:

- Criteria as to whom may be an insolvency representative are objective, clearly established, and publicly available.

- Insolvency representatives are competent to undertake the work to which they are appointed and to exercise the powers given to them.

- Insolvency representatives act with integrity, impartiality, and independence.

- Insolvency representatives, where acting as managers, are held to director and officer standards of accountability, and are subject to removal for incompetence, negligence, fraud, or other wrongful conduct.

Specific Rules and Practices for an Insolvent Bank

In the case of an insolvent bank, the power to manage both the assets and the bank itself is frequently given to bank guarantee funds, which guarantee the interests of creditors, specifically depositors.[6] For example, in Ukraine, a law enacted in September 2012 extended the mandate of the Deposit Guarantee Fund beyond reimbursing depositors of failed banks to acting as their provisional administrator or insolvency representative. Thus, the government agency manages the operations of the failed bank before liquidation is complete and has the power necessary to collect financial and transaction information, identify and collect information on suspicious transactions, cooperate with criminal investigators, and launch civil or commercial lawsuits on behalf of the company to recover funds and other assets.

In other countries, for example, Moldova, the insolvency representative of an insolvent bank is appointed by the central bank or by a supervisory authority. This approach has many advantages, most significantly that the appointed insolvency representative is familiar with banking. The second advantage is that the insolvency representative enjoys legal protection as a central bank employee. This is especially important in a jurisdiction with a corrupt legal system, where debtors can initiate legal suits against the insolvency representative to jeopardize the recovery process. The appointment and remuneration of the insolvency representative by the central bank also solves the problem of an insolvent bank that does not have sufficient funds to pay the insolvency representative's salary.

The insolvency representative appointed by the central bank has the power to initiate civil cases against debtors, former managers, or other third parties if he believes that the bank was affected by their actions (or inaction). In some jurisdictions, the insolvency representative can request that the prosecutor's office initiate criminal cases.

The appointment of an insolvency representative by a central bank was used recently in Moldova after an extensive bank fraud. After the fraud was discovered, the National Bank of Moldova played a key role in the liquidation of the banks, including appointing an insolvency representative, approving significant transactions executed by the insolvency representative, and declaring the liquidation process closed. Three banks were ultimately liquidated, including one of systemic national importance. The former Prime Minister was sentenced to nine years in prison on corruption charges.

Liquidation is not demonstrably more efficient than the use of a Deposit Guarantee Fund in Ukraine for winding up an insolvent bank. Although the administrative resources allocated for the liquidation and recovery process are important, the legal framework determining the powers of the insolvency representative and the functioning of the legal system in practice, which is often related to the level of systemic corruption, are critical.

Effects of the Appointment of an Insolvency Representative

Box 1.6 provides a brief overview of the powers afforded to insolvency representatives in many jurisdictions.

BOX 1.6   Overview of the Powers of an Insolvency Representative

Insolvency representatives are appointed to manage the assets of an institution that has been declared insolvent. They generally have the power to do the following:

- Act on behalf of the bankrupt entity, sometimes jointly with the debtor

- Take possession of assets related to the insolvent entity and manage them

- Gain access to all books, transaction records, accounting documentation, or financial information relevant to the management of the company

- Conduct or order a comprehensive audit of financial statements and suspicious transactions to find information that can lead to recoverable assets

- Use all investigative and provisional measures available in civil litigation, including seizure of property and records, public examination, and freezing of assets

- Exercise discovery and examination of interested parties and third parties

- Compel testimony from individuals, such as directors or managers, and bring claims against them for wrongdoing in any corrupt scheme

- Bring claims against third parties for participating in any wrongdoing

- Act to prevent any further movement of assets out of the insolvent estate.

Once the insolvency process has commenced and an insolvency representative is appointed, an automatic or court-imposed moratorium against any action, execution, or other legal process against the bankrupt person or entity takes effect.[7] If a bankrupt entity has assets within the jurisdiction in which it was declared bankrupt, insolvency regimes will in principle prevent any further movement of assets out of the insolvent estate. The effect of such a moratorium internationally can be complex, but international regimes—such as the Council of the European Union's Regulation on Insolvency Proceedings[8] and the United Nations Commission on International Trade Law (UNCITRAL) Model Law on Cross-Border Insolvency[9]—often give this stay of proceedings extraterritorial effect.

In most insolvency cases, the insolvency representative gets access to all books, transaction records, accounting documentation, and financial information relevant to the company. Often, the insolvency representative will conduct or order a comprehensive audit of financial statements and suspicious transactions to find information that can lead to recoverable assets. These audits are generally the starting point of an investigation, when specific actions or transactions that resulted in the transfer of assets of value out of the company are identified. As representatives of the company or the bankrupt estate, insolvency representatives are able to use all investigative and provisional measures available in civil litigation, including seizure of property and records, public examination, and freezing of assets. In addition, insolvency laws often give the insolvency representative powers of discovery and examination of interested parties and third parties. Government officials seeking to recover assets should remember, however, that conducting forensic investigations and other legal actions can be extremely expensive, and creditors may not support these investigations financially in the absence of a good chance of success. If the chance of success is weak, insolvency representatives can coordinate with law enforcement on transactions that appear suspicious.

Insolvency laws generally authorize the insolvency representative to take possession of and manage assets from the bankrupt individual or company. These powers give the insolvency representative direct access to recoverable property. In most cases, asset recovery is complex, and financial investigations as well as provisional measures are necessary to identify, trace, and secure recoverable funds or property.

Cross-Border Recognition and Conducting Insolvency Actions Abroad

Assets are often hidden in financial centers where local secrecy rules or banking opportunities are abused by criminals. Countries pursuing asset recovery efforts often have to work across borders to identify and repatriate their stolen funds, including in insolvency cases. In criminal cases, law enforcement authorities have tools that facilitate the exchange of information with their foreign counterparts. (See appendix A for country-specific regulations and UNCAC for the international framework governing such cooperation.) Coordination with law enforcement authorities may be useful to insolvency practitioners.

Insolvency representatives who seek to exercise their powers in foreign countries must keep in mind the variations in legal recognition and enforcement of foreign judgments in cross-border insolvency proceedings. Under domestic legislation and applicable multilateral or bilateral treaties, a number of foreign jurisdictions support insolvency representatives appointed in the jurisdiction where the insolvency proceedings were initiated. In the British Virgin Islands, for example, a foreign representative appointed in "relevant countries"[10] may apply to the court for orders to restrain any proceedings against a debtor or in relation to any of the debtor's property, to require any person to deliver any property of the debtor to the foreign representative, and to appoint an interim receiver of any property of the debtor.

In some jurisdictions, courts can recognize foreign bankruptcy proceedings and issue orders at the request of a foreign representative authorized to act on behalf of the debtor. In the Cayman Islands, such orders include prohibiting the commencement of legal proceedings against the debtor, staying the enforcement of a judgment against the debtor, and ordering the turnover to the foreign representative of any property belonging to the debtor. The foreign representative can also request an order requiring a person in possession of information relating to the business of the debtor to be examined and to produce documents.

In other jurisdictions (including the United Kingdom and the United States), cross-border insolvency legislation gives the UNCITRAL Model Law the force of local law. Expert meetings have shown that jurisdictions that adopted this model handled cases quickly and routinely, with no difficult issues. Requests for legal recognition could be resolved within hours.[11] In the United Kingdom, foreign insolvency proceedings and foreign representatives must be recognized by courts if certain formal documents are provided and an application is issued by the Business and Property Courts (Insolvency and Companies List) of the High Court.

Other systems to ensure that insolvency representatives and foreign representatives can exercise the rights and act on behalf of the estate in foreign jurisdictions include the Regulation (EU) 2015/848 on Insolvency Proceedings (Recast Insolvency Regulation), which gives primacy to the law of the country that opens insolvency proceedings if the company has its center of main interest (COMI) in that country. The insolvency representatives are then able to exercise their powers in all other European Union (EU) Member States where assets are located. Regulation 2015/848 also establishes the basis for opening secondary proceedings against businesses located in a Member State that is not the company's COMI. However, there is a premise that in order to enforce foreign insolvency orders in England, foreign representatives must show that the debtor in the insolvency proceeding falls within the existing U.K. common law rules.[12] The case discussed in box 1.7 illustrates the application of this principle. See the section in chapter 5 titled *United Kingdom Cross-Border Insolvency Regulations 2006* for more detail.

In the United States, chapter 15 of the Bankruptcy Code incorporates the Model Law on Cross-Border Insolvency to encourage cooperation between the United States and foreign countries on cross-border insolvency cases (Goffman 2017). Under chapter 15, "foreign representatives" of debtors who have initiated insolvency proceedings abroad,

---

BOX 1.7 U.K. Supreme Court Rules on Cross-Border Insolvencies: The Limits of Universalism in *Rubin v. Eurofinance S.A.*[a]

Eurofinance S.A. created Consumers Trust, an English law trust governed by English law, with a jurisdiction clause selecting English courts. The scheme of Consumers Trust ran into financial difficulties and the Trust decided to seek protection by entering bankruptcy under the U.S. Bankruptcy Code. The U.S. bankruptcy court appointed Rubin, a foreign representative, to serve on behalf of the Trust to seek aid, assistance, and cooperation from the English High Court to enforce the U.S. bankruptcy court's judgments against persons and entities residing in or owning property in the United Kingdom.

In the U.S. bankruptcy court, Rubin commenced proceedings that were equivalent to the insolvency claims under the U.K. Insolvency Act 1986. The defendants, who were not resident in the United States and did not submit to the jurisdiction of the bankruptcy court, did not present a defense in those proceedings.

(continued next page)

Default and summary judgment were entered against them. Rubin then sought to enforce these judgments.

The main issue before the U.K. Supreme Court was whether the English courts would recognize and enforce insolvency orders under common law. By the usual common law rules, for a claimant to enforce a foreign order in the United Kingdom, the defendants would have had to be present in the foreign country at the time proceedings were instituted and to have been a claimant or counter-claimant in the foreign proceedings. They would also have to have participated in the proceedings or submitted to the jurisdiction of the foreign court.

The U.K. Supreme Court held that insolvency proceedings do not form a separate category of judgment outside the common law rules, and foreign officeholders would have to show that the debtor met the criteria under the existing common law rules to enforce foreign insolvency orders in England.[b] The UNCITRAL Model Law (see the section in chapter 5 titled *The UNCITRAL Model Law on Cross-Border Insolvency*), which is implemented by the Cross-Border Insolvency Regulations 2006, makes no mention of the recognition or enforcement of foreign judgments against third parties. Accordingly, the Cross-Border Insolvency Regulations 2006 were not designed to provide for reciprocal enforcement of judgments. Because there is no expectation that foreign courts will mutually enforce U.K. court decisions, existing rules governing courts' common law and statutory powers regarding foreign judicial enforcement are deliberately limited in scope. It is a matter for the legislature, rather than the judiciary, to expand the rules on when foreign insolvency judgments can be enforced in U.K. proceedings. Finally, as a matter of policy, the rules for foreign insolvency judgments should be no more liberal than those for judgments made in proceedings other than insolvency proceedings.

Prior to *Rubin*, the most relevant case law suggested that, in insolvency proceedings, an English court did not have to follow the normal common law rules on enforcing a judgment. *Rubin* returns the law to classic principles on jurisdiction and enforcement. *Rubin* establishes that in order to enforce foreign insolvency orders in the United Kingdom at common law, the foreign office holder must show that the judgment debtor: (1) was present in the foreign jurisdiction at the time the proceedings were instituted; (2) was the claimant or the counter-claimant in the foreign proceedings; (3) had submitted to the foreign proceedings by appearing voluntarily; and (4) had submitted to the foreign proceedings by agreement.

a. Rubin v. Eurofinance S.A. [2012] UKSC 46. For a discussion of the case, see Lexology, "Enforcing Orders Made in Insolvency Proceedings" (October 24, 2012), https://www.lexology.com/library/detail.aspx?g=a2f57317-5f4f-4f19-b5c2-49e9a043f684; Financier Worldwide, "U.K. Supreme Court Rules on Cross-Border Insolvencies" (January 2013), https://www.financierworldwide.com/uk-supreme-court-rules-on-cross-border-insolvencies/#.Wflu9jdqFBr.
b. See Stephanie Woods, Case Comment, "Rubin & Anor v. Eurofinance S.A. & Ors [2012] UKSC 46," U.K. Supreme Court Blog (October 29, 2012), http://ukscblog.com/case-comment-rubin-and-another-respondents-v-eurofinance-sa-and-others-appellants-new-cap-reinsurance-corporation-in-liquidation-and-another-respondents-v-a-e-grant-and-others-as-members-of/.

where the debtor has its COMI, are allowed to seek recognition of the proceedings abroad, as either a foreign main proceeding or a foreign nonmain proceeding in the United States (Goffman 2017). Debtors can block chapter 15 recognition if they offer evidence of corruption in the case against them. A general allegation that the foreign judiciary is corrupt is not sufficient. The case in box 1.8 describes evidence of corruption in a foreign insolvency proceeding that is sufficient to block chapter 15 recognition.

Finally, in those jurisdictions that have not adopted the Model Law, insolvency representatives may have to seek cross-border recognition through the international private law of the country. They may be able to use their power to request specific measures on behalf of the debtor by using existing legislation on asset recovery, civil proceedings, and investigation measures. Insolvency representatives may have to request that the specific measures ordered by the courts where the insolvency proceedings took place be recognized by the courts of the jurisdiction where assets are located. Insolvency representatives may request, directly or by using their own judicial system, the exequatur, or the execution of specific measures using treaties on legal assistance and recognition or execution of court decisions. Generally, this method of securing the extraterritorial effect of insolvency proceedings is time-consuming and uncertain.

BOX 1.8 **U.S. Court Grants Recognition of Former Russian Business Owner's Bankruptcy**

The Commercial Court of the Moscow Region appointed a financial administrator in the insolvency proceeding of Sergey Petrovich Poymanov pursuant to Russian bankruptcy law. In a U.S. bankruptcy court, the administrator moved for recognition of the Russian insolvency proceeding as a "foreign main proceeding" against a Delaware company, PPF Management LLC (PPF), under chapter 15 of the U.S. Bankruptcy Code. Counsel for PPF challenged the recognition of the Russian bankruptcy proceedings against Sergey Poymanov.

PPF alleged extensive corruption in the Russian judicial system but was unable to provide evidence that the Russian insolvency proceeding had been tainted.

In *In re Sergey Petrovich Poymanov*,[a] the U.S. bankruptcy court stated that the bar to block chapter 15 recognition is high, explaining that PPF would have to show that such an order would be manifestly contrary to the public policy of the United States. To do so, PPF would have had to present evidence of corruption in the present case, rather than merely claiming that corruption exists generally in the Russian judiciary. The court said that there was "simply no evidence" of the improprieties, bad faith, and criminal corruption that PPF alleged had tainted the Russian bankruptcy.

a. In re Sergey Petrovich Poymanov, No. 17-10516 (Bankr. S.D.N.Y. July 31, 2017), https://www.leagle.com/decision /inbco20170801684. For a discussion of the case, see "Bid to Block Ch. 15 Recognition Scrutinized in Russian Case," LAW360 (July 19, 2017), https://www.law360.com/articles/946123/bid-to-block-ch-15-recognition -scrutinized-in-russian-case; "Russian Ex-Biz Owner's Bankruptcy Granted U.S. Recognition," LAW360 (August 1, 2017), https://www.law360.com/articles/950228?scroll=1.

In Brazil, despite significant reforms, the law has no provision for the recognition of court decisions issued in foreign insolvency proceedings and does not address cross-border issues (Felsberg n.d., 2–3). The Constitution, the Introductory Law to the Civil Code, and the Code of Civil Procedure of Brazil provide the general rules that require an exequatur for the recognition of foreign judgments (Felsberg n.d., 3). In the absence of detailed rules, recognition and enforcement of foreign judgments of insolvency proceedings are theoretically possible in Brazil under certain conditions (Felsberg n.d., 3). One of the most important conditions for an exequatur to be enforceable in Brazil is the requirement that a foreign judgment be submitted to the Superior Court of Justice (the second highest federal court in the Brazilian judiciary system).[13]

The Swiss Federal Supreme Court ruled that a worldwide freezing order issued by the High Court of London (often still referred to by their former name, Mareva injunctions) could be enforced by Swiss courts.[14] These worldwide freezing orders are generally not enforceable in the United States, although exceptions exist.

Powers of Insolvency Representatives in Asset Recovery

Tools Available to Collect Information and Evidence

Once insolvency representatives have identified and analyzed the suspicious transactions that may lead to stolen or recoverable assets, they will be able to use a range of measures to collect information and evidence to ensure effective asset recovery and bring actions to bankruptcy or other civil courts. These measures will be briefly presented in this section and are discussed in more detail in chapter 2.

The powers of insolvency representatives often include the ability to compel the production of books and records, including from lawyers, accountants, and banks, and to conduct audits. In addition, whether in common or civil law systems, the insolvency representatives, acting on behalf of the insolvent entities, can use existing legal tools to trace, secure, and recover assets.

In civil cases, such tools include disclosure and "no-say" or "gag" orders (especially in common law jurisdictions), search orders, freezing orders, and proprietary injunctions. Witness interrogations can be used to pursue civil corruption cases. Provisional measures may include worldwide freezing orders (Mareva injunctions) and similar measures.

Initiating criminal proceedings by reporting transactions to law enforcement authorities may also be an effective tool for collecting evidence of fraudulent activity, identifying assets, and enforcing judgments. The use of the criminal law provides prosecutors with the power to compel third parties to provide material that may be relevant to their investigation or prosecution; this material may also reveal the existence or amount of assets. In many jurisdictions, particularly common law jurisdictions, a complainant (who may be an insolvency representative acting on behalf of an insolvent entity) has a constitutional or common law right to commence a private prosecution.

Insolvency representatives should consider a range of criminal offenses for a criminal prosecution. For example, many individuals and companies seek voluntary arrangements with their creditors to avoid the scrutiny that follows from insolvency. When submitting a voluntary proposal, debtors have an obligation to provide accurate and truthful information. Failure to do so is a criminal offense, for which an insolvency representative or complainant may bring a criminal prosecution to compel the sharing of information and documents from third parties that may reveal evidence and assets.

Legal Actions that Authorize Insolvency Representatives to Claim Assets

Once insolvency representatives have identified recoverable assets and collected evidence to prove their cases in court, they can use a number of different legal actions to obtain effective recovery orders. This section provides a brief overview of these tools; more details are discussed in chapters 2 and 3.

Asset Tracing and Other Proprietary Claims

In general, insolvency representatives can assert a proprietary interest over a company's misappropriated assets. Misappropriation may result from various activities, including embezzlement, bribery, abuse of power, and theft. Claims may also extend to any subsequent assets into which the original property was converted. In court, the plaintiffs will need to show enough evidence to conclude that assets are derived from the debtors. In many common law jurisdictions, the concept of "beneficial ownership" allows courts to apply the theory of "constructive trust" when third parties have paid bribes to agents of principals. Under the theory of constructive trust, the bribes paid to agents are considered to be the proceeds of the breach of a fiduciary duty. The insolvency representative will be able to claim that the state is the beneficial owner of the funds or of the assets purchased with the bribes.[15]

Actions on the theory of constructive trust generally do not exist in civil law countries, which may hinder the recovery of bribes that never become property of the state. Plaintiffs may need to use personal claims instead to recover the funds (Brun et al. 2015, 51–55). The insolvency representatives in civil law countries will also be able to exercise "revindication" actions to recover embezzled or stolen assets. Some of these actions may be outside the scope of the insolvency law and may need to be sought in the broader legal system, such as in the civil courts.

Claims Available to Void, or Avoid, Suspicious or Fraudulent Transactions

The ability to cancel transactions that took place before the insolvency of the enterprise is an important tool for asset recovery in corruption cases. Such transactions may be fraudulent, gratuitous, preferential, or outside the ordinary course of business. Many countries' insolvency frameworks provide for a look-back or suspect period—a timeframe close to the company's insolvency during which payments are presumed to be preferential. The suspect period in most developed jurisdictions (such as France, Italy, Spain, the United Kingdom, and the United States) is no longer than two years prior to the commencement of the insolvency process (Gurrea-Martinez 2016, 21). Preferential payments can involve a debtor's transfer to a creditor for an existing debt or, as the result of the transaction, a creditor's receiving a share of its claim from the debtor's assets higher than that received by other creditors of the same class or rank. The suspect period is often longer for transfers to affiliated persons (that is, those with a family or corporate relationship) or are gratuitous (consisting of payment with no proper consideration). Additional detail is provided in chapter 3. Box 1.9 presents the World Bank Principle on Avoidable Transactions.

Some jurisdictions focus on voiding, or avoiding, fraudulent, dishonest, or undervalued transactions, and other jurisdictions have specific provisions allowing or facilitating the avoidance of transfers made by the debtor within a certain period before the bankruptcy filing.

An action for a declaration of invalidity, which restores the assets of the debtor, is usually brought by the administrator, the legal representative, the commissioner for the execution of the plan, or the public prosecutor. In some jurisdictions, specifically in common law systems, insolvency representatives may apply for a broader range of remedies. Courts often have discretion as to the types of remedies, including undoing transactions in whole or in part, or ordering compensation or any measure that would restore the debtor to the position it would have had had it not entered into the transaction.

If a country's insolvency legislation does not enable insolvency representatives or creditors to look back at transactions that occurred close to the time of insolvency and cancel them, the insolvency representative may have difficulty acquiring resources that were dispersed prior to the insolvency. Some insolvency legislation does not clearly define a voidable transaction. Therefore, it is important to develop a clear understanding of what the legislation and case law of a country has determined constitutes a voidable

---

BOX 1.9 **World Bank Principle C11: Avoidable Transactions**

C11.1 After the commencement of an insolvency proceeding, transactions by the debtor that are not consistent with the debtor's ordinary course of business or engaged in as part of an approved administration should be avoided (cancelled), with narrow exceptions protecting parties who lacked notice.

C11.2 Certain transactions prior to the application for or the date of commencement of the insolvency proceeding should be avoidable (cancelable, including fraudulent and preferential transfers made when the enterprise was insolvent or that rendered the enterprise insolvent).

C11.3 The suspect period, during which payments are presumed to be preferential and may be set aside, should be reasonably short in respect to general creditors to avoid disrupting normal commercial and credit relations, but the period may be longer in the case of gifts or when the person receiving the transfer is closely related to the debtor or its owners.

transaction before using this method, even if it is broadly available within the legislative framework. Further discussion of preferential and fraudulent transactions is found in chapter 3 in the sections titled *Proceedings for Fraudulent or Wrongful Trading* and *Preferences and Transactions at Undervalue*, which describe specific mechanisms for recovery of stolen assets and provide examples of how they have been used.

Undervalued transactions or preferences are not necessarily proof of corruption, but, when corruption is suspected, they should be investigated to determine whether corporate entities are being used to conceal the value and the beneficial ownership of money flows.

Liability Actions

In some jurisdictions, the insolvency representative or the public prosecutor can carry out actions against legal (or de facto) directors when, at the date of the commencement of the bankruptcy case, the assets of the debtor are not sufficient to pay the company's liabilities. Courts can hold a director liable for all or part of the difference based on evidence that the position of the creditors has deteriorated following the misconduct (whether mismanagement or fraud) of the director. In France, insolvency representatives may have to show that the mismanagement or fraud has directly caused an increase in liabilities that contributed to the insufficiency of assets. As in typical tort cases, insolvency representatives must demonstrate fault (mismanagement, fraud, or any action that should not have been performed by a normally diligent director), damages (insufficiency of the assets or an increase in the shortfall of assets), and causation (the damages were caused by the fault) to sustain the claim. Winning a judgment of personal liability against directors requires a good deal of evidence of gross negligence or dishonesty, and we emphasize the point. Negligence or dishonesty of directors is sometimes obvious, especially in cases in which directors agree to abuse companies they manage to enable corruption or money laundering. For example, there may be evidence that a company was created for the purpose of buying and managing real estate purchased with proceeds of corruption on behalf of a corrupt official. For more information, see chapter 3.

Piercing the Corporate Veil

In principle, a registered corporation is a legal entity separate from those who own or control it. Shareholders, managers, directors, or beneficial owners of a company are generally not liable for the expenses or debts incurred by it. In some legal systems, however, legislation or courts may find it appropriate to "pierce the corporate veil" and to treat the rights or liabilities of a company as the rights or liabilities of its shareholders, directors, or agents. This is particularly relevant when the company was created or used as a device or a façade for fraud or money laundering. The company may be placed under receivership or another insolvency proceeding if it cannot or will not pay judgments or other debts arising from the fraudulent activities conducted by its shareholders, directors, or beneficial owners. In these circumstances, it will be possible for insolvency representatives to recover assets legally owned either by the entity or its shareholders, directors, and beneficial owners. (See the section titled *Piercing the Corporate Veil* in chapter 3.)

Key Points from this Chapter

- The purpose of an insolvency proceeding is to seize and sell assets of the debtor-defendant and distribute the money equitably to creditors and other injured parties, thus protecting their rights.

- In insolvency proceedings, certain jurisdictions allow a business to be wound up on just and equitable grounds, which can be valuable in cases of corruption, embezzlement, or any type of fraudulent activity. Other jurisdictions rely on more traditional definitions of insolvency.

- Insolvency representatives can, through their efforts to retrieve assets of the estate, recover illegally obtained proceeds stolen by corrupt officials.

- In the pursuit of assets stolen for corrupt purposes, insolvency representatives have a variety of tools available to them to identify and immobilize assets belonging to the insolvent estate.

- Some corruption crosses borders; insolvency representatives are often called upon to exercise their powers in foreign countries, where they must keep in mind the variations in the legal rules for recognition and enforcement of foreign judgments in insolvency proceedings.

Notes

1. Just and equitable grounds is generally a common law concept; although the concept is not clearly defined in many legislative frameworks that provide for it, it has evolved through case law. For example, in the United Kingdom, winding-up orders have been made when a company was formed for fraudulent purposes. See, for example, Anglo-Greek Steam Co. [1866] LR 2 Eq 1; In re West Surrey Tanning Co. [1866] LR 2 Eq 737; In re London and County Coal Co. [1867] LR 3 Eq 355.
2. See, for example, In re International Securities Corp. [1908] 99 LT 581.
3. In Belgium and France, prosecutors can petition a court to open a bankruptcy proceeding. In the United Kingdom and the United States, only a creditor may petition to open a case.
4. If a country has no or very limited rules and regulations for who can become an insolvency representative, the quality and reliability of those representatives will vary. Moreover, should a country not have a mechanism for monitoring and training representatives, holding them to account and ensuring continued quality will be difficult.
5. In the private-professional model, the primary obligation is the recovery of assets for creditors and injured parties. In the public model, the employee has a state salary, so the incentives are slightly different.
6. Some countries have insolvency laws that exclude financial institutions from their scope and application. In this section, we focus on countries that include them.

7. The moratorium can sometimes be initiated as early as the filing of the originating insolvency process.
8. Regulation (EU) 2015/848 of the European Parliament and of the Council of May 20, 2015, on Insolvency Proceedings (Recast Insolvency Regulation).
9. Forty-four jurisdictions have adopted the Model Law on Cross-Border Insolvency.
10. The "relevant countries" are Australia, Canada, Finland, Hong Kong SAR, China, Japan, Jersey, New Zealand, the United Kingdom, and the United States.
11. UNCITRAL-INSOL-World Bank Report, 12th Multinational Judicial Colloquium, Sydney, March18–19, 2017. http://www.uncitral.org/pdf/english/colloquia/insolvency-2017/twelfthJC.pdf.
12. See case comment at https://www.lexology.com/library/detail.aspx?g=b952eefc-e9c9-4687-b9a9-3950f0db4e02.
13. Brazil will not recognize foreign courts' rulings, however, if the law provides for exclusive Brazilian jurisdiction (Felsberg n.d., 3).
14. Swiss Federal Supreme Court, 94A_366/2011 (October 31, 2011).
15. For example, in *Attorney General v. Reid*, the government of Hong Kong SAR, China was recognized as the owner of properties purchased with bribes because the funds were obtained through a breach of fiduciary duty. The dishonest official was deemed to hold the funds (and the properties purchased with them) as a constructive trustee; the government was their true owner. Similarly, in *Kartika Ratna Thahir v. Pertamina* (Singapore), https://star.worldbank.org/corruption-cases/sites/corruption-cases/files/documents/arw/Pertamina_Singapore_Appeals_Court_Aug_25_1994.pdf, an Indonesian state-owned energy enterprise sued its former executive to recover bribes he received from two contractors. The former executive had deposited the bribes in a bank in Singapore. The court found that the former executive owed a fiduciary duty to the enterprise and that he held the bribes as a constructive trustee for the true owner.

References

Brun, Jean-Pierre, Pascale Helene Dubois, Emile van der Does de Willebois, Jeanne Hauch, Sarah Jais, Yannis Mekki, Anastasia Sotiropoulou, Katherine Rose Sylvester, and Mahesh Uttamchandani. 2015. *Public Wrongs, Private Actions*. Washington, DC: World Bank.

EBRD (European Bank for Reconstruction and Development). 2007. "EBRD Insolvency Office Holder Principles." EBRD, London. https://www.ebrd.com/documents/legal-reform/ebrd-insolvency-office-holder-principles.pdf.

———. 2014. "Assessment of Insolvency Office Holders: Review of the Profession in the EBRD Region." EBRD, London.

Felsberg, Thomas Benes. n.d. "Cross-Border Insolvency in Brazil: The Need for Rules." Unpublished.

Goffman, Jay M. 2014. Panel discussion at the International Insolvency & Restructuring Symposium: America Now!, London, October 30–31.

Gurrea-Martinez, Aurelio. 2016. "The Avoidance of Pre-Bankruptcy Transactions: An Economic and Comparative Approach." Working Paper Series 10/2016, Instituto Iberomaericano de Derecho y Finanzas (IIDF), Madrid, Spain.

UNCITRAL (United Nations Commission on International Trade Law). 2004. *Legislative Guide on Insolvency Law*. New York: UNCITRAL.

World Bank. 2016. "C17: Insolvency of International Enterprise Groups." In *Principles for Effective Insolvency and Creditor/Debtor Regimes*. Washington, DC: World Bank.

2. Investigative Measures Potentially Available in Insolvency and Civil Cases

International insolvency and cross-border asset recovery efforts to combat corruption entail complicated processes. To right the wrongs and ensure that the culprits do not enjoy their illicit gains, investigators charged with investigating corruption or misappropriation in insolvency proceedings need both judicial and nonjudicial resources.

Experienced investigators of corruption are accustomed to using both, enabling them to develop a complete picture, target available resources, and form a plan. In cases of corruption, nonjudicial tools, such as investigative measures and examination of witnesses, can be crucial in establishing the purported insolvency that leads to the appointment of an insolvency representative, who can then assist in the recovery of assets. Chapter 2 provides an overview of the various tools available to professionals charged with recovering the proceeds of corruption.

Investigative measures to identify and trace assets that could be the proceeds of corruption and targets for civil actions are available in both civil law and common law jurisdictions. Depending on the legal system, litigants, including insolvency representatives acting on behalf of the insolvent entity, can exercise powers provided for by commercial or civil legislation or insolvency legislation, including obtaining court orders authorizing disclosure of information and searches of premises. This chapter lays out the range of legal tools using examples drawn primarily from common law systems.

Many of these tools exist under different names and concepts in other legal systems. For instance, authorization to search private premises in the course of civil litigation can be granted by French judges through application of the French Code of Civil Procedure. Policy makers and practitioners in different legal systems should investigate the legislation and jurisprudence in their jurisdictions that might enable them to reach solutions similar to those described in this chapter.

Extrajudicial Investigative Tools

In addition to the investigative measures available in an insolvency case, meaningful information can be gathered through extrajudicial investigative activities, including:

- Examination of all available records and other documentary evidence
- Liaison with known sources of information, both open and confidential, including sources within official police and government circles when appropriate
- Attempts to develop additional confidential and open sources

- Covert gathering of intelligence and evidence
- Retrieval of pertinent information from various electronic and other databases
- Surveillance of principal targets and, if appropriate, potential targets
- Initiation of covert evidence and intelligence gathering and the commencement of discreet inquiries to accomplish, among other things, the reverse tracing of concealed assets
- Interviews with selected witnesses.

Overt, extrajudicial investigative activities, coupled with judicially assisted investigations, when appropriate, may be used to develop information on the assets and ultimate beneficial ownership of entities that may have been used to move, conceal, or hold assets that were corruptly obtained.

Information relevant to building a case is often available online, including judgments, liens, and bankruptcy filings; property records; business registrations (cross-referenced in various ways); oil and gas partnerships; motor vehicle and drivers' license registrations; regulatory proceedings and filings; thoroughbred horse ownership; lists of all former addresses; property tax rolls; information relating to divorce proceedings; and details of boat or plane ownership. Social media are also powerful sources of public information.

Discovery Databases as a Source of Information

Search engines can locate and decipher information that may appear insignificant to the untrained eye. Asset recovery investigations require access to computer records and analysis of digital information. The programs available to assist an investigator are potentially helpful but complex. Computer forensic professionals will be needed.

Computer databases were an invaluable tool for the investigative team that searched for dormant accounts left by Holocaust victims in Swiss banks. A team of dedicated accountants combined old-fashioned investigative methods with the capabilities of a large relational database to find and sort through reams of files and recover almost $1 billion in funds deposited by individuals who died in Nazi-era concentration camps. These funds were placed in escrow to pay claims brought by lawful heirs.

Electronic evidence has often shaped the outcome of high-profile insolvency and civil asset recovery investigations, ranging from the theft of intellectual property and insider trading that violates U.S. Securities and Exchange Commission (SEC) regulations to proof of employee misconduct that results in termination of employment for cause. Critical electronic evidence is often found in a suspect's web-browsing history in the form of received emails, sites visited, and attempted Internet searches.

What is saved on a computer hard drive can provide invaluable information, but often what is not saved—or to be more precise, what has been deleted—will prove critical. Often a hard drive retains information that a user has tried to delete; computer professionals may be able to retrieve this information.

Examination of Witnesses under Standard Insolvency Practices

Insolvency laws often specify the duties and functions of insolvency representatives upon their appointment and the powers available to them to perform those duties and functions efficiently and effectively.

Insolvency representatives are generally empowered to conduct examinations of witnesses who may have information likely to assist the representative in determining the state of affairs or assets of a debtor, whether in a personal or corporate insolvency.

Obtaining information concerning the debtor, its assets, liabilities, and past transactions (especially those taking place during the period immediately preceding the commencement of insolvency or bankruptcy) is one of the core duties of the insolvency representative. The powers available to obtain that information generally include examining the debtor and any third person who had dealings with the debtor.

In the United Kingdom, insolvency representatives may make application to the court for orders against any officers of the company or any persons whom they think capable of providing information concerning the business, dealings, and affairs of the company.

An English court enjoys unfettered discretion whether to issue the order, but the exercise of that discretion involves a balancing of the needs of insolvency representatives against any possible oppression, unfairness, or prejudice to examinees. The process of examination is not intended to enable the representatives to, nor will they be permitted to, conduct a "fishing expedition." Courts might also, in the exercise of their discretion, consider the risk of collusion between the insolvency representatives and the debtors' management, resulting in a settlement that isn't in the best interest of the creditors.

Targets of Examination

Examination powers are generally used to inspect or obtain documents from directors; in most jurisdictions, other persons and entities—including a company's solicitors, accountants, auditors, and bank managers—may also be examined if they are believed to have information about the business, dealings, and affairs of the company. In applying for examination power with regard to a particular person, the onus is on the insolvency representative to establish a reasonable need for the information sought. Relevant information may be held by individuals and corporate entities, as well as governmental bodies.

In a corporate insolvency that consists of a winding up in the United Kingdom, an examinee could be:

- Any officer or director of the company
- Any person known or believed to have in his or her possession any property of the company or any person supposed to be indebted to the company
- Any person whom the court believes capable of giving information about the promotion, formation, business, dealings, affairs, or property of the company.

In a bankruptcy (personal insolvency) in the United Kingdom, an examinee could be:

- The bankrupt person or his or her spouse or former spouse
- Any person known or believed to have in his or her possession any property belonging to the estate of the bankrupt person or any person supposed to be indebted to the bankrupt person
- Any person whom the court believes capable of giving information about the bankrupt person or his or her dealings, affairs, or property.

Although corporate insolvency processes would be initiated where the company maintains its center of main interest (COMI), personal insolvency cases are likely to be initiated within the debtor's home jurisdiction. Therefore, it is less likely that a personal insolvency, as opposed to a corporate insolvency, would take place in an offshore jurisdiction.

In the United Kingdom, the power of examination is not restricted to persons situated or resident there. Questions of jurisdiction and recognition of the order may arise, however, when an examination order is sought against a foreign entity. In some cases, a foreign court may be willing to grant to a recognized foreign insolvency representative powers that are the same or equivalent to those available to local insolvency representatives. Box 2.1 provides an example of how a court in Australia, which has adopted the United Nations Commission on International Trade Law (UNCITRAL) Model Law, dealt with a request for assistance from a British Virgin Islands court.

The examination of corporate officers is considered less likely to be oppressive than an examination of third parties, because officers have a statutory duty to cooperate and, by virtue of their position, are more likely to be in possession of relevant information.

Generally, no examination will be permitted once the insolvency representative has commenced or has resolved to commence legal proceedings against the person in question, because such information would ordinarily come to light in the process of discovery during those proceedings.

Whether the examination of a person outside the jurisdiction will be ordered depends on the statutory mechanisms available in the forum or local jurisdiction and in the target jurisdiction. Courts generally have no power to summon a foreign resident. In the United Kingdom, section 237(3) of the Insolvency Act 1986 provides that persons who are not within the jurisdiction (but could be summoned to appear before the court under section 236 of that Act) may be subject to an order for examination either within or outside the United Kingdom. Section 236, which deals with inquiries into a company's dealings, does not have extraterritorial effect.

If an appropriate mechanism for such an order exists in the jurisdiction in which the examination target resides, however, an English court may make such an order under section 237(3) of the Act.[1] Applications to obtain information from foreign residents can be technically complex. Expert advice is often needed in such situations.

BOX 2.1

Crumpler ex rel. Global Tradewaves Ltd. v. Global Tradewaves, in re Global Tradewaves Ltd.[a]

The applicants (Crumpler) had been appointed as insolvency representatives of Global Tradewaves Ltd. (Global Tradewaves), a company registered in the British Virgin Islands pursuant to an order of the Eastern Caribbean Supreme Court's High Court of Justice, the British Virgin Islands Commercial Division (the British Virgin Islands Court).

Even though there was no evidence that Global Tradewaves carried on business in Australia or had any Australian creditors, its insolvency representatives sought recognition in an Australian court of the British Virgin Islands liquidation as a foreign main proceeding. The insolvency representatives also sought an ancillary order that a former director of Global Tradewaves be summoned for examination.

The Federal Court of Australia was satisfied that the statutory winding-up regime that operates in the British Virgin Islands is similar to that of the Australian Corporations Act and, accordingly, that the liquidation of Global Tradewaves was a foreign proceeding and that its insolvency representatives were foreign representatives. The court was also satisfied that the British Virgin Islands was the COMI of Global Tradewaves.

Recognition of the British Virgin Islands liquidation enabled the insolvency representatives to seek ancillary orders for the examination of the former director, who they believed was resident in Australia.

A public examination of the former director could be ordered on three bases:

- Article 21(1)(d) authorized the court to provide for the examination of a witness on information concerning the company's assets, affairs, rights, obligations, or liabilities.

- Article 21(1)(g) authorized the court to make an order for a public examination pursuant to division 1 of part 5.9 of the Corporations Act.

- Having received a letter of request from the British Virgin Islands Court, the court also had discretion to order an examination under section 581 of the Corporations Act.

The court was satisfied that the former director was a person likely to have an intimate knowledge of the affairs of Global Tradewaves and that the insolvency representative was entitled to summon the former director for public examination.

a. [2013] FCA 1127.

Range of Examination

In practice, an examination is confined to information concerning the corporation's promotion, formation, management, administration, winding up, or any other affairs of the corporation or related entities. Questions concerning matters relating to the "property" of a corporation are also within the ambit of an examination. In theory, this could extend to any potential right to compensation for malfeasance of its officers, including its directors, and the general right of action for breach of directors' duties.

The range of an examination must be seen in the context of assisting insolvency representatives in carrying out their duties. To enable creditors to be repaid, insolvency representatives are required to take possession of, protect, liquidate, and distribute the assets or the proceeds of the liquidation of the assets of the debtor to the creditors, in accordance with applicable statutory priorities. To fulfill those functions, insolvency representatives must determine what assets exist, both tangible and intangible. Determining what assets are available will invariably involve obtaining information about such assets from those in a position to provide it, such as bank managers, accountants, officers, even business associates or affiliated persons or entities. Insolvency representatives may use powers of examination to obtain information from those who are unwilling to provide it voluntarily.

In *Re Gold Co. Ltd.*, Sir George Jessel, referring to a section that provided for the power to examine, wrote:

> [T]he whole object of the section is to assimilate the practice in winding up to the practice in bankruptcy, which was established in order to enable assignees, who are now called trustees, in bankruptcy to find out facts before they brought an action, so as to avoid incurring the expense of some hundreds of pounds in bringing an unsuccessful action, when they might, by examining a witness or two, have discovered at a trifling expense that an action could not succeed.[2]

Justice Buckley, in *Re Rolls Razor Ltd.*, wrote, in relation to the comparable provision in the Companies Act 1948 (U.K.):

> The powers conferred by [section] 268 are powers directed to enabling the court to help an insolvency representative to discover the truth of the circumstances connected with the affairs of the company, information of trading, dealings, and so forth, in order that the insolvency representative may be able, as effectively as possible and, I think, with as little expense as possible and with as much expedition as possible, to complete his function as insolvency representative, to put the affairs of the company in order and to carry out the liquidation in all its various aspects, including, of course, the getting in of any assets of the company available in the liquidation.
>
> It is, therefore, appropriate for the insolvency representative, when he thinks that he may be under a duty to try to recover something from some officer or employee of a company, or some other person who is, in some way, concerned with the company's affairs, to be able to discover, with as little expense as possible and with as much ease as possible, the facts surrounding any such possible claim.[3]

Any question designed to elicit information concerning assets of the debtor, even intangible assets or assets that have been misappropriated, should fall within the range of the examination. Information that may enable the insolvency representative to reach an informed decision also falls within the scope of what is considered permissible.

In general, an examination will be permitted as long as an insolvency representative is not seeking information merely to pressure a potential litigation adversary for an improper purpose. An applicant who seeks an examination order for the purpose of obtaining a forensic advantage not otherwise available, however, may be committing an abuse of process.

Use of Information

Information obtained during an examination can be used only to further the exercise of the functions and duties of insolvency representatives. The nature, scope, and purpose of their power are relevant to how the information will be used. As long as the information is sought for a proper purpose, examinees, particularly officers and former officers and directors of the debtor, have no privilege against self-incrimination when responding to requests for information. The answers provided, however, may not be used in criminal proceedings.

Even in the absence of a privilege against self-incrimination, the maintenance of confidentiality is an important consideration. Information that comes from third parties may be subject to privacy protection and secrecy provisions, such as those applicable to banks. The insolvency representative is generally permitted to use that information only for the insolvency proceeding in which the examination was permitted, unless the court decides otherwise. Confidentiality issues may also be relevant to the provision and obtaining of information in criminal proceedings against the debtor.

It is a general principle of law that the use of information or material obtained under compulsion authorized by statute is limited by the provisions of the statute.

In *Johns v. Australian Securities Commission*, a case concerning statutory powers of investigation conferred on the police, Justice Brennan wrote:

> [W]hen a power to require disclosure of information is conferred for a particular purpose, the extent of dissemination or use of the information disclosed must itself be limited by the purpose for which the power was conferred. In other words, the purpose for which a power to require disclosure of information is conferred limits the purpose for which the information disclosed can lawfully be disseminated or used. In *Marcel v. Commissioner of Police of the Metropolis*, Sir Nicolas Browne-Wilkinson V.-C. said, in reference to a statutory power conferred on police to seize documents: "Powers conferred for one purpose cannot lawfully be used for other purposes without giving rise to an abuse of power. Hence, in the absence of express provision, the Act cannot be taken to have authorized the use and disclosure of seized documents for purposes other than police purposes."[4]

These principles apply in insolvency investigations. The use of the information obtained is generally confined to enabling the insolvency representative to locate, preserve, and liquidate assets for the benefit of creditors, or to take any other steps in furtherance of those objectives.

Insolvency representatives who become aware of activity that might constitute a fraud on the company may pursue information that may ultimately lead to the institution of proceedings against those involved. Thus, in carrying out asset recovery in a case of corruption, insolvency representatives could seek an examination of any persons likely to have information regarding the acts of corruption themselves, the location of any proceeds of corruption, and the identity of any persons who facilitated those acts, whether the corruption itself or the assistance in laundering the proceeds.

Costs of Examination

Examinees may be ordered to pay the costs of the insolvency representative's application if they are ordered to produce assets as a result of an examination, evidence contained in an affidavit, or the production of documents. Examinees may also be ordered to pay the costs of an examination if they unjustifiably refuse to provide the information sought. Some jurisdictions impose criminal sanctions in more serious cases of withholding of information.

Discovery

Discovery (sometimes called "disclosure") refers to the process of obtaining information within the context of pending proceedings. Discovery may be requested from the opposing party or, in certain circumstances, from third parties to the litigation. Discovery of information is generally limited to information relevant to the issues between the parties. When the pleadings in a case have made clear what facts are at issue, discovery can be sought, and ordered, to produce the information necessary to determine the truth. Pleadings set out the basis of the case; they must be as clear and comprehensive as possible.

Nonstatutory Tools

Anton Piller (Search and Seizure) Orders

The *Anton Piller* (search and seizure) order takes its name from a decision of the English Court of Appeal in *Anton Piller K.G. v. Manufacturing Processes Ltd.*[5] It permits the applicant's solicitors to enter premises, without notice, and to search for and remove all items covered by the order. The usual purpose of an *Anton Piller* order is to preserve evidence or property. Although not commonly used in civil or insolvency cases, an *Anton Piller* order may be available.

In insolvency cases, an *Anton Piller* order is particularly useful when an insolvency representative has reason to believe that documents or property belonging to a debtor, or concerning a debtor, its affairs, or its assets, may be destroyed. It may be used against lawyers, accountants, and other service providers who may possess information relevant to the debtor's assets and business. Because such orders are executed without notice, the potential for concealment or destruction of records prior to the arrival of the insolvency representative is reduced.

In *Anton Piller*, Lord Justice Ormrod of the English Court of Appeal set out the following requirements for granting this form of relief:

- There must be an extremely strong prima facie case against the respondent.
- The damage, potential or actual, to the applicant must be very serious.
- There must be clear evidence that the respondents have in their possession relevant documents or property and that there is a real possibility that they may destroy such material before an inter partes application can be made.

The Court of Appeal also laid out safeguards against abuse of *Anton Piller* orders and placed the responsibility on the applicant's solicitors for ensuring that the orders are carried out meticulously and carefully with the greatest respect for the defendants' rights.

In recognition of the drastic nature of the relief and its potentially serious consequences, courts have developed further safeguards to prevent injustice.

In *Universal Thermosensors Ltd. v. Hibben*,[6] the Chancery Division laid down the following guidelines for the execution of an *Anton Piller* order:

- Orders should be executed on working days during normal office hours to ensure that the defendant has access to legal representation.
- A detailed record of materials or property removed at the time of execution of the order must be made.
- The solicitor executing the order should be neutral and experienced (in serving and executing the order, there should be a supervising solicitor present who should explain the order to the defendants and give them the opportunity to consult their own solicitors. If the defendants wish to apply to discharge the order as having been improperly obtained, they must be allowed to do so. If the defendants refuse permission to enter or to inspect, the plaintiff must not force its way in. It must accept the refusal and bring it to the court's attention, if need be, on an application to commit for contempt of court).
- The order should be carried out in the presence of the defendant or his representative.
- Where the premises are likely to be occupied by an unaccompanied woman, if the supervising solicitor is a man, he must be accompanied by a woman.

Further, in *Canadian Bearings Ltd. v. Celanese Canada Inc.*[7] in 2006, the Canadian Supreme Court laid down the following additional safeguards:

- The scope of an *Anton Piller* order should not be wider than necessary, and material that is not spelled out in the order should not be removed.
- The number of persons who are to execute the search should be limited, and their names should be specified in the order.
- The order should state explicitly that the defendant is entitled to return to court on short notice to discharge the order.

- The order should contain a limited-use clause stating that the documents seized may only be used for the pending litigation.
- A list of all evidence seized should be prepared and provided to the defendant for inspection and verification at the end of the search and before the removal of the evidence.
- If a list of evidence cannot be provided to the defendant at the time of the search, the documents seized should be placed in the custody of the independent supervising solicitor.

In the United Kingdom, the High Court's power to grant search and seizure orders (*Anton Piller*) is derived from section 7(1) of the Civil Procedure Act 1997, and the relevant procedural requirements are set out in *Civil Procedure Rule 25* and *Practice Direction 25A*.

Common law jurisdictions that permit this type of relief include Australia, India, Ireland, Jersey and other British common law financial centers, and New Zealand. Similar relief is also available in Belgium, France, and Germany, and, for the enforcement of intellectual property rights, throughout the EU.[8]

Norwich Pharmacal *(Disclosure) Orders in Common Law Jurisdictions*

United Kingdom and commonwealth courts have jurisdiction to grant prelitigation discovery orders known as *Norwich Pharmacal* orders, based on common law and equitable principles. In the English case that gave this order its name—*Norwich Pharmacal v. Customs and Excise Commissioners*[9]—Norwich Pharmacal Co. (Norwich) owned the patent for a chemical compound that was being illegally imported without a license by unknown third parties. Norwich wanted to identify the third parties to take action against them. Norwich brought a court action against defendants known to have records of the importers to force them to disclose the importers' identities. The court granted the order, stating that, although usually only parties to litigation have an obligation to disclose, the defendants had a duty to assist Norwich, the party who was wronged, by giving it any information that could identify the wrongdoers.

Lord Reid formulated the jurisdiction as follows:

> The [authorities] seem to me to point to a very reasonable principle that if through no fault of his own a person gets mixed up in the tortious acts of others so as to facilitate their wrongdoing he may incur no personal liability *but he comes under a duty to assist the person who has been wronged by giving him full information and disclosing the identity of the wrongdoers.* I do not think it matters whether he became so mixed up by the voluntary action on his part or because it is his duty to do what he did. It may be that if this causes him expense the person seeking information ought to reimburse him. But justice requires that he should cooperate in righting the wrong if he unwittingly facilitated its perpetration.[10]

The jurisprudence on disclosure orders has been extensively developed.[11] The categories of cases in which the order may be granted are neither closed nor confined to litigation. For example, in *CHC Software Care v. Hopkins & Wood*,[12] Justice Mummery ordered a firm of solicitors to disclose the names and addresses of persons to whom a letter making allegedly false allegations had been sent to enable CHC to write to the same persons correcting the alleged false statements.

The English Court of Appeal recently clarified the circumstances under which *Norwich Pharmacal* relief is available in *NML Capital Ltd. v. Chapman Freeborn Holdings Ltd.* While recognizing the need for flexibility in *Norwich Pharmacal* jurisdiction, to avoid its becoming "wholly unprincipled," the Court of Appeal said that it was essential for the third party to be "involved in the furtherance of the transaction identified as the relevant wrongdoing."[13]

Omar & Ors, R (on the application of) v. Secretary of State for Foreign & Commonwealth Affairs[14] clarified that *Norwich Pharmacal* jurisdiction may not be used to obtain information for use in a foreign proceeding if the foreign jurisdiction has a statutory process for obtaining evidence. The court dismissed the application, finding that the English courts do not have jurisdiction to order the provision of evidence for foreign proceedings using *Norwich Pharmacal* orders if the provision of that evidence is prohibited by the Evidence (Proceedings in Other Jurisdictions) Act 1975:

> [T]he power of the courts to use *Norwich Pharmacal* proceedings must, in our view, be developed within the confines of the existence of the statutory regime through which evidence in proceedings overseas must be obtained. *Norwich Pharmacal* proceedings are not ousted, but where proceedings, such as the present proceedings, are brought to obtain evidence, the court as a matter of principle ought to decline to make orders for the provision of evidence, as distinct from information, for use in overseas proceedings.
>
> ....
>
> In our judgment it matters not that there may be no procedure in Uganda for obtaining evidence from the UK to be used in those courts.[15]

This approach was confirmed more recently in *Ramilos Trading Ltd. v. Buyanovsky*,[16] in which the court also emphasized that *Norwich Pharmacal* relief would not be ordered to further a fishing expedition.

Although *Norwich Pharmacal* jurisdiction is no longer considered exceptional and has been used in many common law jurisdictions, the approach to granting the relief is not always consistent. Some jurisdictions, such as Ireland, will permit discovery only to identify the wrongdoer, not to obtain factual information concerning the alleged wrong.[17] Other jurisdictions have not confined the information to the identity of wrongdoer only.

Norwich Pharmacal orders cannot be obtained against persons who are likely to be witnesses (or are prima facie defendants) in any proceeding instituted on the basis of an alleged wrong. This was reemphasized in *Hilton v. D IV LLP*.[18] In his judgment, Judge Pelling, Q.C., referred to the statement of principle in the speech of Lord Reid in

Norwich Pharmacal as the origin of the jurisdiction. He highlighted, however, Lord Reid's limitations on the use of the jurisdiction:

> [Lord Reid noted that:] "It is not available against a person who has no other connection with the wrong than that he was a spectator or has some document relating to it in his possession." He pointed out that "the reason why the respondent in those proceedings was treated differently was because "without certain action on their part the infringements could never have been committed." It was these qualifications that led Lord Reid to formulate the principle that the claimants seek to rely on in this case in these terms: "[I]f through no fault of his own, a person gets mixed up in the tortious acts of others so as to facilitate their wrongdoing he may incur no personal liability but comes under a duty to assist the person who has been wronged by giving him full information." However, as Lord Reid said in *Norwich Pharmacal*, "information cannot be obtained by discovery from a person who will in due course be compellable to give that information . . . on a subpoena duces tecum." Hence the remedy, which is an exceptional procedural device made available to avoid injustice, is available only against those who won't or shouldn't be liable for the wrong but have nevertheless become mixed up in its commission. Outside that limited class the remedy is not available.[19]

Credit Suisse Trust v. Intesa San Paulo SpA and Banca Monte dei Pasche di Siena[20] was the first reported case of an English court ordering *Norwich Pharmacal* disclosure against two London branches of an Italian bank, even though the banking activity took place in Italy and all the information sought was held in Italy. Credit Suisse had obtained a judgment in Guernsey against a customer of Intesa and Banca Monte for dishonest breach of fiduciary duty. Credit Suisse took steps to enforce that judgment and to obtain further information about the client's assets.

The key question was whether the Italian banks could be forced to disclose information about the client's assets, because the relevant banking activity took place in Italy and was therefore governed by Italian law, in particular, Italian banking confidentiality rules. The evidence before the judge in respect of Banca Monte was that its London branch was able to access the relevant information in Italy so as to ensure compliance with the order being sought. The availability of evidence from Intesa's London branch was less clear.

The judge held that, because this was a fraud case, there was nothing in earlier case law to prevent him from making an order merely because the information sought was held by the banks in Italy. The court found that Banca Monte was willing to provide at least some of the information but considered that an order of the English court might be necessary to protect it from Italian confidentiality laws. With respect to Intesa, the judge believed that if Banca Monte's London branch was able to obtain the information from Italy, it should be possible for Intesa's London branch to do so. The judge was also aware that, if either Banca Monte or Intesa did not comply, Credit Suisse would not pursue those banks in England for contempt of court. Rather, Credit Suisse would apply to have the Guernsey judgment or the English *Norwich Pharmacal* order, or both, recognized in Italy. On that basis, the judge granted the *Norwich Pharmacal* relief against the London branches of the two Italian banks.

Norwich Pharmacal relief will not be ordered if the information is sought for the purpose of obtaining an advantage in another litigation, as opposed to enabling the bringing of a suit. In *Orb A.R.L. v. Fiddler*,[21] Mr. Justice Popplewell discharged a *Norwich Pharmacal* order that he had made previously, ruling that the information had not been sought for legitimate purposes but to discredit a party in a separate litigation to obtain an advantage in that case. The judge also found that there were several breaches of the duty to make full and frank disclosure that would have been sufficient to discharge the order.

When preaction disclosure is sought but the facts do not necessarily support *Norwich Pharmacal* relief, court rules of procedure in a particular jurisdiction might be interpreted to provide it. In Jamaica, for example, although there is no specific rule or procedure providing for preaction discovery, such as an equivalent to Civil Procedure Rule Part 31 in the United Kingdom, the Supreme Court of Judicature in *Clarke v. Bank of Nova Scotia Jamaica Ltd.*[22] held that the existing rules gave the court jurisdiction to make orders for discovery even before a case had been filed (see box 2.2).

Similarly, if an applicant presents a prima facie case that his funds have been subject to fraud or other misappropriation, and that the funds or their proceeds have been paid by or through the bank or other entity from which disclosure is sought, a *Bankers Trust*

BOX 2.2   *Clarke v. Bank of Nova Scotia Jamaica Ltd.*

In *Clarke v. Bank of Nova Scotia Jamaica Ltd.*,[a] the Supreme Court of Judicature in Jamaica referred to rule 8.1(5) of the Civil Procedure Rules, which permits the filing of an application for a remedy before proceedings have started, that is, before a claim form has been filed. The application must be made pursuant to part 11 of the Civil Procedure Rules, which, in part, authorizes the court to exercise any power which it might exercise at a case management conference. The court noted that a court has many powers in a case management conference and that rule 27.9(1)(a) obliges a court to consider whether to give directions for standard disclosure and inspection. Rule 28.6(2) allows a court to order specific disclosure on or without application, and rule 28.6(3) allows an application for specific disclosure to be made at a case management conference. The court's assessment of these rules was, among other things, that they conferred jurisdiction to make orders for discovery even before a claim has been filed.

The court further concluded that rule 17.2 (which governs the grant of interim remedies) allowed the making of preclaim orders for inspection, detention, and preservation of relevant property.

The Supreme Court of Judicature also disagreed with the proposition that *Norwich Pharmacal* jurisdiction is not applicable when the target of discovery is itself a wrongdoer, highlighting a difference of approach to this particular question across jurisdictions.

a. [2012] JMCA Civ 8.

order can be used to require a bank to disclose relevant banking documentation.[23] In most British international financial centers (such as Jersey), the courts will issue broad disclosure orders against third parties if necessary to plead a claim, trace assets, or enforce a judgment, or if disclosure is in the interest of justice.

Ancillary Sealing and Gagging Orders

Common law courts (and many civil law courts) have the power to seal a court's file and prohibit the disclosure of the fact or nature of its orders. Ancillary orders sealing the court record and "gagging" persons with knowledge of it (preventing them from disclosing the existence or subject matter of the proceedings) are complementary to an order permitting the proceedings to be heard in camera (in private). A court must be able to enforce its own rules of practice and to guard against any abuse of its processes. Publication of the fact or details of proceedings to locate and identify concealed assets (or to identify the beneficial ownership of companies holding assets) may enable an apparent wrongdoer to take steps to put those assets beyond the claimant's reach.

An ancillary secrecy order—a compulsory nondisclosure order against a bank or offshore company formation agent under the protection of utmost secrecy—is one of the most powerful tools available to an insolvency representative or other claimant searching for concealed assets or proof of their ultimate beneficial ownership. If a dishonest debtor or corrupt politician has no notice of the gathering of his or her bank and company ownership secrets, assets may be effectively found and frozen.

In *Connelly v. DPP*,[24] Lord Morris of Borth-y-Gest explained the jurisdiction:

> There can be no doubt that a court which is endowed with a particular jurisdiction has powers which are necessary to enable it to act effectively within such jurisdiction. I would regard them as powers which are inherent in its jurisdiction. A court must enjoy such powers in order to enforce its rules of practice and to suppress any abuses of its process and to defeat any attempted thwarting of its process.[25]

The power to order that proceedings be sealed or that all those with knowledge of those proceedings be prohibited from disclosing the fact or details thereof must be weighed against the principle that justice must be administered in public. Article 6(1) of the European Convention on Human Rights and Fundamental Freedoms (ECHR) provides: "In the determination of his civil rights and obligations or of any criminal charge against him, everyone is entitled to a fair and public hearing within a reasonable time by an independent and impartial tribunal established by law. Judgment shall be pronounced publicly . . . ." (ECHR 1950).

Furthermore, Article 10 of the ECHR guarantees the right of freedom of expression, which may also be infringed by a prohibition on the disclosure of information. A significant overriding interest must justify any restriction on the publication of proceedings or the principle of open justice. The issue of a court's jurisdiction to anonymize and restrict publication of its proceedings was considered by the U.K. House of Lords in *Scott v. Scott.*[26] Viscount Haldane, Lord Chancellor, stated:

> While the broad principle is that the Court of this country must, as between parties, administer justice in public, this principle is subject to apparent exceptions such as those to which I have referred. But the exceptions are themselves the outcome of yet a more fundamental principle that the chief object of the Courts of Justice must be to secure that justice is done.[27]

Viscount Haldane then went on to explain the necessity of protecting the subject matter of litigation as a justification for restricting publicity in a particular class of proceedings. He stated:

> The other case referred to, that of litigation as to a secret process, where the effect of publicity would be to destroy the subject matter, illustrates a class which stands on a different footing. There it may well be that justice could not be done at all if it had to be done in public. As the paramount object must always be to do justice, the general rule as to publicity, after all only a means to an end, must accordingly yield.[28]

Marcus A. Wide v. FirstCaribbean International Bank[29] provides an example of extensive sealing and gagging relief (see box 2.3).

Ex parte discovery provides access to information that the other party is not yet aware has been disclosed. It thus may provide significant strategic and tactical advantages.

BOX 2.3   *Marcus A. Wide v. FirstCaribbean International Bank*[a]

Marcus A. Wide, insolvency representative of Tradex Ltd. (a company in liquidation), which had been involved in a widespread Ponzi scheme, instituted a long series of ex parte applications in The Bahamas; Belize; Dominica; Jamaica; Québec, Canada; Singapore; and the United States in an effort to recover assets of Tradex that had been misappropriated and concealed in various jurisdictions. The investigation of the affairs of Tradex required an extensive multijurisdictional investigation and court proceedings.

Mr. Wide was able to show that the results of the investigations were likely to be rendered worthless if the existence of the investigations and the proceedings was disclosed. (There was no countervailing interest on the part of Tradex to trump the necessity for the secrecy orders.) Wide obtained a series of disclosure orders accompanied by gag and seal orders at various stages of the proceedings, including an order that the court's file and record be sealed and all parties be prevented from disclosing either the fact of the application or the content of the pleadings, except as necessary to seek advice from legal counsel. The duration of these orders was then extended as necessary by the courts involved until Mr. Wide was in a position to freeze the assets found through the disclosure orders obtained and the investigations conducted. Thousands of bank, company formation, and other confidential records were accumulated over the course of two years of judicially sanctioned secret investigative activity. Millions of dollars of assets were discovered and frozen.

a. 2005/Com/bnk 21 (unreported).

It is of the greatest benefit when knowledge by the opposing party that the discovery is being conducted could lead to evasive action, which would have a detrimental effect on the chances of the party seeking discovery to satisfy its claim.

In common law jurisdictions, a court may grant an ex parte disclosure order on the basis of common law or equitable principles. The jurisdiction exists separate from the rules for discovery prescribed by the applicable rules of court procedure or the civil procedure rules of the jurisdiction concerned.

Other Investigative Tools

Mareva Injunctions and Mareva by Letter in Common Law Jurisdictions

A number of common law jurisdictions provide for worldwide freezing orders called *Mareva* injunctions. These freezing orders originated in *Mareva Compania Naviera S.A. v. International Bulkcarriers S.A.*[30] and have been codified in section 37 of the U.K. Supreme Court Act 1981. These orders may be granted to prevent defendants from removing assets from a jurisdiction or otherwise disposing of them.

Mareva by letter notifies a third-party guardian or holder of assets, such as a bank, that those assets may be subject to a constructive trust. It informs the holder of the assets that their beneficial owner is not the account holder of record but rather a defrauded entity or government and advises them of their potential civil or criminal liability if it permits any transfer or disposal of those assets. *Mareva* by letter will generally dissuade a bank from transferring the funds until the case is resolved or until the funds are formally frozen following a court order. Informing a bank that it is being used for fraudulent activity and is therefore vulnerable to private or public legal action may cause it to prevent the funds' release or further misuse. The *Mareva* by letter procedure should be accompanied by criminal or civil actions on behalf of the fraud victim.[31]

Freezing Orders in Civil Law Jurisdictions

Legal tools to seize or freeze assets are also available in civil law jurisdictions. In France, for example, the Code des Procédures Civiles d'Exécution (CPCEx) addresses potential civil remedies in asset recovery cases. In particular, article L.111-1 provides that any creditor is entitled to a provisional measure to ensure that his rights are respected. Similarly, article L.511-1 provides for temporary seizure of assets: a claimant may request, ex parte, a freeze on assets belonging to the defendant if the assets exist and are believed to be in danger of dissipation. The procedure is very informal; the claimant has to bring a request to a judge, who can grant a provisional order to seize the assets. A proprietary injunction covers the property or the traceable proceeds of the property (the proprietary assets) of the defendant and prohibits dealing in those assets. The claimant has to present a credible case and must demonstrate that it is just and convenient for the judge to grant the order. The risk of dissipation of the funds need not be proved separately because the defendant is holding the claimant's assets. An almost identical action called "embargo preventivo" is available under Argentina's Code of Civil and Commercial Procedure.

Discovery in Aid of Foreign Proceedings

Asset-related information is generally readily available in the United States. Section 1782 of the U.S. Code empowers courts to permit any interested party to obtain discovery for use in foreign proceedings from a person located in the judicial district, even if this evidence could not be accessed under the rules of the foreign proceeding.[32] When considering an application under section 1782, a U.S. district court may also consider: (1) whether the person from whom discovery is sought is a party to the foreign proceeding; (2) the nature of the foreign tribunal and the character of the foreign proceeding; (3) whether the request is an attempt to circumvent evidence-gathering restrictions or policies in the foreign jurisdiction; and (4) whether the request is unduly intrusive or burdensome.[33]

For litigants outside the United States, section 1782 provides a quick, efficient, and relatively inexpensive method of obtaining evidence within the United States. Although most foreign countries provide for procedures enabling the gathering of evidence from foreign witnesses, or witnesses abroad, section 1782 is designed to provide foreign litigants the opportunity to obtain discovery of documents or tangible evidence located in the United States. Effectively, all the foreign litigant needs to establish is that, if the parties against whom discovery is sought were located within the foreign jurisdiction in which the underlying proceedings are taking place, the applicant could seek the same discovery relief they seek in the U.S. district court. The only reason the applicant comes for relief to the U.S. district court (as opposed to the foreign court) is that the evidence sought is not physically available to the applicant in the foreign jurisdiction.

Under section 1782, a court order for discovery may be made upon the application of any "interested person." Section 1782 does not require an interested person to first seek discovery from the foreign or international tribunal or that judicial proceedings be pending at the time assistance is sought. The fact that an interested person is contemplating bringing proceedings abroad is sufficient. Discovery under section 1782 is pre-action discovery. The determination of whether to grant assistance under a section 1782 application hinges not on whether the proceeding is pending but on whether the requested discovery will likely be of use in a foreign judicial proceeding (or whether it will likely lead to the discovery of admissible evidence). Section 1782 provides a flexible procedure for the taking of depositions in aid of foreign proceedings. The section is supplemented by safeguards in the U.S. Federal Rules of Civil Procedure, particularly rules 26–32, which are designed to prevent misuse of the section.

The application is made to the U.S. district court in the location of the residence of the party from whom the evidence is sought. The application is based on an affidavit of the applicant, who must be an interested person, that is, a party to the anticipated foreign litigation. A person may not be compelled to give testimony or a statement or to produce documents or other items in violation of any legally applicable privilege. If an issue of discoverability is raised during the section 1782 application proceedings, the primary burden falls upon the applicant to make a showing that the information is discoverable under foreign law.[34]

Key Points from this Chapter

- Investigations may be conducted to develop information on the location of assets and the beneficial ownership of entities that are believed to have been used to move, conceal, or hold assets that were corruptly obtained.

- Information relevant to building a case is often available online or in virtual databases.

- Insolvency representatives are typically empowered to conduct examinations of witnesses who may have in their possession information likely to assist the representative in determining the state of affairs or assets of a debtor.

- Search and seizure orders may be available and particularly useful when an insolvency representative believes that relevant documents or property belonging to a debtor may be destroyed.

- Commonwealth courts have jurisdiction to grant prelitigation discovery orders known as Norwich Pharmacal orders, based on common law and equitable principles.

- Worldwide freezing orders (Mareva injunctions) inform asset holders (such as banks) that the beneficial owner of assets is not the account holder of record but a defrauded entity or government and advise them of their potential liability in the event of any transfer or disposal of the assets in question.

Notes

1. See MF Global UK Ltd. (In Special Administration) [2015] EWHC 2319 (Ch) (July 31, 2015).
2. [1879] 12 ChD 77 (CA) 85.
3. [1968] 3 All ER 698, 700.
4. [1993] 178 CLR 408, 423–24.
5. [1976] Ch. 55 (CA).
6. [1992] 1 WLR 840.
7. [2006] 2 R.C.S.
8. See Directive 2004/48/EC of the European Parliament and of the Council of April 29, 2004, on the Enforcement of Intellectual Property Rights.
9. [1974] AC 133.
10. Ibid., § 175B-C (emphasis added).
11. In *Clarke v. Bank of Nova Scotia Jamaica Ltd.* (see box 2.2), the Supreme Court of Judicature in Jamaica disagreed with the proposition that *Norwich Pharmacal* jurisdiction does not apply when the target of discovery is itself a wrongdoer.
12. [1993] FSR 241.
13. [2013] EWCA Civ. 589.

14. [2012] EWHC 1737 (Admin) (June 26, 2012).
15. Ibid.
16. [2016] EWHC 317.
17. See Megaleasing UK Ltd. v. Barrett [1993] I.R.L.M. 497, 504 (Chief Justice Finlay) ("The remedy should be confined to cases where very clear proof of a wrongdoing exists and possibly, so far as it applies to an action for discovery alone prior to the institution of any other proceedings, to cases where what is really sought is the names and identity of the wrongdoers rather than the factual information concerning the commission of the wrong.").
18. [2015] EWHC 2 (Ch) (January 12, 2015).
19. [1974] AC 133, 174.
20. [2014] EWHC 1447 (Ch) (March 6, 2014).
21. [2016] EWHC 361 (Comm) (February 26, 2016).
22. [2012] JMCA Civ. 8.
23. The *Bankers Trust* order comes from *Bankers Trust v. Shapira* [1980] 1WLR 1274.
24. [1964] AC 1254.
25. Ibid., 1301.
26. [1913] AC 417.
27. Ibid., 437.
28. Ibid.
29. 2005/Com/bnk 21 (unreported). See Peter Maynard and Colin Jupp. 2015. "Judicial Secrecy and Suspension of Adversarial Proceedings: Super-Injunctions, Sealing and Gagging as Effective Tools." https://www.ibanet.org/Article/NewDetail .aspx?ArticleUid=47185731-d747-4417-9c4b-d032df155b62.
30. [1975] 2 Lloyd's Rep. 509 (CA).
31. The fraud victim may obtain proprietary injunctions or the appointment of an insolvency representative at the same time as the *Mareva* by letter to prevent movement of the funds before the bank agrees to take steps to freeze the assets. The danger in not taking some form of injunctive relief at the same time as the *Mareva* by letter is that the defendant is on notice, but the bank has not been forced to act immediately. If the bank does not agree to take steps to prevent the movement of the funds, the defendant may transfer the money out of the reach of the victim.
32. 28 U.S.C. § 1782 (2019).
33. Intel Corp. v. Advanced Micro Devices, Inc., 542 U.S. 241 (2004).
34. In re Asta Medica S.A. 981 F.2d 1 (1st Cir. 1992).

Reference

ECHR (European Court of Human Rights). 1950. *European Convention on Human Rights.* Strasbourg: Council of Europe.

3. Identifying Insolvency and Receivership Targets and Other Liable Persons in Corruption Cases

Bribe Takers and Related Entities

The fight against corruption has gained momentum and is now a global initiative. Several jurisdictions have taken steps to strengthen their frameworks and mechanisms for the return of assets derived from corrupt activities by criminalizing and listing corruption as a predicate offense for money laundering.

In cases of bribing foreign officials and embezzling public funds in developing jurisdictions, however, there may be difficulties in any investigation seeking corruption proceeds. The proceeds are typically hidden abroad or laundered using overseas intermediary services provided by lawyers, accountants, or company formation agents. In the United Kingdom, for example, a recent Transparency International UK report found that as of 2016, 44,022 London land titles were owned by overseas companies; 91 percent of overseas companies owning London property did so through holding companies in offshore jurisdictions, known as "secrecy jurisdictions," that don't require beneficial ownership to be public; 986 land titles had links to politically exposed persons (PEPs)[1]; and over 75 percent of them were owned by companies based in the British Virgin Islands or Panama.[2] Over £180 million worth of property in the United Kingdom has been subject to criminal investigation as the suspected proceeds of international corruption.

Although the United Nations Convention Against Corruption (UNCAC) is explicit about the need to criminalize both bribe paying and receiving, many legislative provisions focus only on the bribe payer. For example, neither the U.K. Bribery Act nor the U.S. Foreign Corrupt Practices Act (FCPA) generally imposes liability on the public official who is the recipient of a bribe.[3] There are, however, many civil law jurisdictions that criminalize bribe taking.

Though most legislation focuses primarily on bribe payers, especially in common law countries, law enforcement has the ability to prosecute bribe takers. The lack of awareness by local law enforcement that such practices are occurring, and how they occur, contributes significantly to the relative impunity of bribe takers.

Official data on the enforcement efforts of the parties to the Anti-Bribery Convention were made public for the first time in the 2009 Annual Report of the Anti-Bribery

Convention Working Group (OECD 2009). The Working Group has been collecting data from its members on investigations, proceedings, and sanctions, distinguishing sanctions upon conviction (or a similar finding of culpability for administrative and civil proceedings) from agreements to resolve proceedings without a conviction (or a similar finding of culpability for administrative and civil proceedings), with or without court approval. The data collected distinguish foreign bribery misconduct from other related offenses—in particular, accounting misconduct relating to the bribery of foreign public officials or attempts to conceal bribery—and, where relevant, track cases against individuals and entities separately.

The lack of any, or any effective, investigation to uncover the identity and activity of bribe takers is among the reasons for the relatively small number of cases in which bribe takers are punished or the proceeds of bribery are confiscated. Investigation of foreign bribery is even more difficult because it is likely to involve at least three jurisdictions: (1) the source jurisdiction of the bribe payer; (2) the destination jurisdiction of the bribe taker; and (3) any intermediary jurisdiction(s) used to launder the proceeds.

The main focus of multilateral conventions has been the pursuit of bribe payers. The fewer the bribe payers, the fewer the bribe takers. However, targeting the bribe takers should also be an integral part of any initiative to tackle corruption. Resources must be made available to investigate the demand side of the corruption equation, identifying those that take and those that assist the takers.

In an insolvency proceeding, bribe takers could be identified and targeted using the insolvency representative's powers to identify persons, natural and legal, who have received a benefit at a company's expense. In some common law jurisdictions, a company that is a bribe taker or recipient can be placed into insolvency to be wound up on just and equitable grounds because the company exists only to receive the bribe. The winding up is not a result of liabilities exceeding assets, but is a measure to remedy the wrong of corrupt activity. Corrupt actors use companies for various purposes, including as a conduit for tainted funds or as a repository. Directors of those companies may be nominees, and the truth may be further obscured by the use of companies or trusts standing in as shareholders. Companies have been wound up on just and equitable grounds on the basis of illegality of object and the failure of substratum (box 3.1).

A company that has been formed for an illegal purpose has no substratum. The only opportunity to trace and recover proceeds of corruption may be through gaining control of receiving companies. In Canada; Hong Kong SAR, China; Malaysia; and Singapore, as well as a number of offshore jurisdictions including the British Virgin Islands, the Cayman Islands, and Guernsey, courts can appoint a provisional insolvency representative to conduct an investigation without notice to the real parties in interest. The English courts also have jurisdiction to appoint provisional insolvency representatives. Some jurisdictions specifically provide for the appointment of an insolvency representative for a foreign-domiciled company, depending upon where the company does business. For example, English courts have jurisdiction to wind up a company incorporated abroad if it has "sufficient connection" with the United Kingdom, such as that the company has assets in England, a director is resident there, or if company insurance policies have been placed through the London market (McLachlan and Loizou 2017).

The U.S. Federal Bureau of Investigation (FBI) has increased its efforts to tackle the demand side of foreign bribery—corruption and kleptocracy, in which state officials steal large sums of money from their country's coffers—a problem that has often been left to the foreign countries in which corrupt officials operate. The FBI and the U.S. Department of Justice's (DOJ) Asset Forfeiture and Money Laundering Section have been focusing on kleptocracy through the Kleptocracy Asset Recovery Initiative. In July 2016, the DOJ initiated the largest ever kleptocracy-related asset forfeiture action, in which $1 billion of assets were seized in Switzerland, the United Kingdom, and the United States.[4] The FBI has set up international corruption squads in Los Angeles,

Miami, New York, and Washington, DC, to investigate violations of the FCPA, including acts of kleptocracy and money laundering. The squads will investigate both the supply and demand sides of international corruption.

Bribe Payers and Related Entities

Although bribe payers are specifically targeted by laws such as the U.K. Bribery Act and the FCPA, fines of any size are unlikely to be effective against an insolvent company that cannot pay. Bribers often pay bribes through intermediaries, which then disappear. Intermediaries that are convicted of bribery often have no resources to pay fines. Insolvency processes can prove useful in this scenario. An intermediary company that has been funded for the purpose of paying a bribe but is subsequently rendered insolvent can be placed into liquidation; the insolvency representative can investigate the acts of corruption, identify the beneficiaries of the transaction on both the supply and demand sides, and recover monies paid.

These powers can also be used to investigate other intermediaries, which can lead to identification of the real parties in interest. Furthermore, such investigations can be conducted in secret to protect their integrity and ensure that those responsible and those who benefit cannot frustrate the process.

Agents and Other Facilitators

Agents and facilitators (such as lawyers, accountants, banks, and other intermediaries) can also be targeted through the insolvency process. In the United Kingdom and common law countries, an insolvency representative can discover the identity of agents or facilitators that have assisted an insolvent company in committing the act of corruption itself or in laundering the proceeds, either through statutory powers of investigation or by making application for a *Norwich Pharmacal* order to identify all known or unknown agents, facilitators, or other persons or entities who either knowingly colluded or were unknowingly used by the debtor.

Applications for *Norwich Pharmacal* orders can be made in any jurisdiction in which it is believed information on such facilitators may be located. If such powers are not available to an insolvency representative in a particular jurisdiction, recourse can be had to *Norwich Pharmacal* relief in common law jurisdictions where assets or defendants are located. (For a more detailed discussion of *Norwich Pharmacal* orders, see the section in chapter 2 titled *Norwich Pharmacal (or Disclosure) Orders in Common Law Jurisdictions*.)

Actions by an insolvency representative against a company's directors may extend to a director's corrupt acts, whether or not they benefit the company. Involving a company in criminal conduct or other wrongdoing is a breach of the duties of a director. Similar actions may be brought against others who facilitate the criminal conduct, such as auditors who fail to report or notice a pattern of criminal conduct.

A debtor company may not have the right, however, to bring an action against a third party accused of facilitating corporate wrongdoing. The in pari delicto (in equal fault) defense can sometimes preclude the insolvency representative from pursuing a cause of action against the facilitator on the company's behalf if it is alleged that the debtor company participated in the wrongdoing. In the United States, the debtor company may be charged with the acts of the officer implicated in the wrongdoing under the "corporate imputation" doctrine (known as the "corporate identification" doctrine in Canada and the United Kingdom).[5] Corrupt conduct might be argued to have been in the best interests of the company if it produced an advantageous result. Similar arguments have been made in U.S. bankruptcies with respect to claims against senior officers of a corporate debtor, and some courts take a short-sighted view of "benefit": even if the benefit is short-lived and harm ultimately ensues, it is nonetheless deemed to be a benefit (see box 3.2).

BOX 3.2	*Kirschner v. KPMG LLP and Teachers' Retirement System of Louisiana v. PricewaterhouseCoopers, LLP*[a]

These cases, decided together by the Court of Appeals of New York, arose from certified questions from the U.S. Court of Appeals for the Second Circuit and the Supreme Court of Delaware regarding the application of the in pari delicto doctrine and the adverse interest exception under New York law.

In *Kirschner*, the CEO of the corporate debtor Refco created a falsely positive picture of Refco's financial condition, which had short-term benefits but ultimately resulted in Refco's filing for bankruptcy under chapter 11. Refco's subsequently formed litigation trust brought suit against Refco's auditors, law firm, and the investment banks involved in Refco's leveraged buy-out and initial public offering for failing to detect the fraud. The district court dismissed the claims against these third-party professionals, holding that they were barred by the in pari delicto doctrine under New York law because the fraudulent acts of Refco's president and CEO were imputable to the corporation.[b]

In *Teachers' Retirement System*, a derivative (shareholder) action was brought in the Delaware Court of Chancery on behalf of AIG alleging that AIG's senior officers fraudulently inflated AIG's financial performance to deceive investors, and that AIG's auditor, PricewaterhouseCoopers was negligent in failing to detect the fraud. The court of chancery concluded that the claims were barred under New York law because the actions of AIG's senior officers were imputable to AIG and, by extension, the derivative plaintiffs.[c]

The New York Court of Appeals held that self-interest does not trigger the adverse interest exception because the wrongdoing in these cases provided short-term benefits to the debtors before the fraud was exposed. Those benefits consisted of, among other things, enabling the raising of funds, attracting customers, or completing acquisitions. The court defended its reasoning thus: "To allow a corporation to avoid the consequences of corporate acts simply because an employee performed them with his personal profit in mind would enable the corporation to disclaim, at its convenience, virtually every act its officers undertake."[d]

a. Kirschner v. KPMG LLP, 15 N.Y.3d 446, 938 N.E.2d 941 (2010).
b. Kirschner v. Grant Thornton LLP, 2009 WL 1286326 (S.D.N.Y. April 14, 2009).
c. In re American International Group Inc., 965 A.2d 763 (Del. Ch. 2009).
d. Kirschner v. KPMG LLP, 15 N.Y.3d 446, 938 N.E.2d 941.

Commissions paid to agents or facilitators pursuant to an agreement to pay a bribe are recoverable by an insolvency representative because the agreements are illegal and therefore void. Again, however, such causes of action can be met with the defense of in pari delicto. The availability and application of this defense varies from jurisdiction to jurisdiction, and a fuller discussion of this evolving area of law is beyond the scope of this publication.

Strategic and Tactical Considerations

Actions against bribe takers, agents, or facilitators, and investigations to identify such persons, can be costly. A lack of funds may severely restrict an insolvency representative's options for pursuing recovery. Some creditors may be willing to fund litigation or take assignment of claims. An insolvency representative may also be able to procure external funding, such as third-party litigation funding, if permitted by the legal system in which the insolvency is supervised. The ability to fund investigations or actions against suspected facilitators is significant and intertwined with the degree of likelihood of success and the ability to recover. Insolvency representatives may need to address, among other things: (1) the choice of insolvency forum when more than one is available; (2) the choice of forum for independent actions for either discovery in respect of, or relief against, facilitators or recipients; (3) the availability of defenses to claims against facilitators in a particular jurisdiction; and (4) the availability and location of assets against which to enforce any judgments against facilitators or recipients.

A chain of intermediaries may each have received some benefit. The cost of pursuing individuals must be weighed against the benefit to be achieved. Very often, the middlemen have few resources, and they may be more useful as sources of information than as sources of asset recovery. Depending upon the size and geographical reach of the acts of corruption, their willingness to divulge valuable information may be tempered by a fear of reprisals. Insolvency representatives must also be aware of the risk that investigations may be sabotaged, may lead down intentionally false paths, or may be met with threats of retaliation. When the stakes are high, as they are in large corruption schemes, corrupt actors may be willing to go to great lengths to protect their interests, sometimes including kidnappings, extortion, and death threats.

Claims against Corporate Officers, Agents, and Third-Party Facilitators

In *Official Receiver v. Wadge Rapps & Hunt*,[6] the House of Lords referred to the dual purpose of a winding up—not just settlement of liabilities and distribution of surplus but also the holding to account of persons responsible for the company's demise. Lord Walker of Gestingthorpe explained that:

> winding up has and has had almost throughout the history of company law, a dual purpose. One purpose is the orderly settlement of a company's liabilities and the distribution of any surplus funds, prior to the company being dissolved. The other is the investigation and the imposition of criminal and civil sanctions in respect of misconduct on the part of persons (especially directors of an insolvent company in compulsory liquidation) who may be shown

to have abused the privilege of incorporation with limited liability. The first function is primarily a concern of a company's creditors and shareholders; the second function serves a wider public interest.[7]

The primary objective of an insolvency representative is to maximize the value of a debtor's estate for the benefit of its creditors. Maximizing value in winding-up cases entails not only the management and sale of tangible assets but also the monetization of intangibles, including potential claims for damages against persons who have diminished or enabled harm to the debtor's estate. These claims are considered "property" and belong to the estate because they represent wrongs against the estate that caused, facilitated, or prolonged the damages to the creditors and victims of the fraud. Such causes of action may lie against directors and other officers, agents, and those who have facilitated wrongs against the debtor such as banks, law firms, accounting or auditing firms, and company formation agents.

Substantial value can be recovered from damages claims directed against third-party facilitators and agents who have enabled the public corruption or the secondary costs of laundering or concealing its proceeds. This value can exceed what may be recovered in traditional assets (such as bank deposits, real estate, or investment securities) from primary targets such as state officials or bribe payers. The use of insolvency proceedings to facilitate the development and prosecution of tertiary damages claims against enablers of corruption or of the laundering of its proceeds can substantially expand the potential recovery for a state that has suffered damages caused by corruption.

For example, in the United States, following the discovery of two of the largest Ponzi schemes in history, the DOJ was able to recover almost $2 billion in bank fines in the New York–based Madoff scheme and may recover several million dollars from Swiss banks in the Houston-based Stanford Financial Group scheme, all of which are to be paid to victims of the respective frauds. Similarly, the U.S. receiver and the Antiguan foreign joint insolvency representatives in the Stanford scheme have reached multimillion-dollar settlements against some law firms and other third parties and continue to litigate significant claims against banks, law firms, and others.

Insolvency law can be used by a victim state to step into the shoes of intermediary companies used by corrupt officials or businessmen, enabling an insolvency representative to take charge of causes of action vested in a company whose assets have been stripped from it by its "controlling minds" with the assistance of banks, lawyers, accountants, or directors who served the company and who may be held to account (see box 3.3).

The Duties of Directors and Managers of Companies

Statutory causes of action vary from jurisdiction to jurisdiction. Many are simply codifications of preexisting law. In the majority of jurisdictions, directors and managers of corporate entities owe duties of care and loyalty to the entity that they manage. Although the specific duties and how they may be enforced vary, the duty of care generally requires that directors and managers exercise the degree of care that ordinarily careful and prudent people would use in similar circumstances. The duty of loyalty requires

Federal Republic of Brazil and Municipality of São Paulo v. Durant International Ltd. and Kildare Finance Ltd.

The facts of this case can be found in box I.1. Brazil and São Paulo had to prove that Durant International Ltd. (Durant) and Kildare Finance Ltd. (Kildare) knowingly received the proceeds of the fraud, or dishonestly assisted in the fraud, or both, to hold them legally responsible. "Knowing receipt" means that the company had knowledge of the fraud. "Dishonest assistance" means that the companies themselves were dishonest in their assistance. A corporation is a legal entity, separate from the people who run it, and therefore it is considered to have its own "mind." The court in Jersey had to decide who was the controlling mind of the companies. A company usually acts through its board of directors and the officers and management who carry out the day-to-day activities. Paulo Maluf had never been a director of the companies. The directors included, among others, a Swiss investment manager and, for a time, Maluf's son Flavio. The court did not, however, look only at the board of directors. It sought to determine who was the company's controlling mind and decided it was Paulo Maluf. The companies had been established on his instruction and for his benefit. He was in control. The knowledge of shadow directors and the people who truly control a company can be attributed to the company, and the company can be held liable on the basis of their actions, in this case, the actions of Paulo Maluf.

a. [2015] UKPC 35.

directors and managers to act in good faith in the best interests of the corporation and its shareholders and to refrain from engaging in activities that might damage the corporation or enable them to receive an improper personal benefit arising from their relationship with it. This would include, for example, a duty not to receive secret commissions. The duty of loyalty also encompasses a prohibition on self-dealing and the usurpation of corporate opportunities by directors. Most, if not all, jurisdictions acknowledge that directors have some form of fiduciary duty, derived from the principle that directors are required to act in the best interests of the corporation and its shareholders.

In cases involving public corruption, companies are almost inevitably used as intermediaries to launder and retain the proceeds of bribery or misappropriation of state assets. The directors and officers (as well as the individuals who control the company, directly or indirectly, or who are de facto directors) of such companies may be sued by an insolvency representative for breaches of their fiduciary duties if such companies are placed into insolvency, and, for example, those individuals are found to have participated in a scheme to use the companies as vehicles to launder or conceal stolen state assets.

Directors must be able to make business decisions without the fear of being held to account, however, if those decisions ultimately cause damage to the company.

Therefore, many jurisdictions permit an element of leeway or discretion. In the United States, for example, under the "business judgment rule," the directors of a corporation are presumed to have acted on an informed basis, in good faith, and in the honest belief that the action taken was in the best interests of the company. Any party challenging the decision in question bears the burden of establishing facts that rebut this presumption. Equivalents or variants of the business judgment rule exist in most jurisdictions. However, the parameters and application of such rules vary considerably. An insolvency representative who seeks to challenge the actions or decisions of an officer or director may argue that insolvency is itself proof of the violation of the business judgment rule. Nonetheless, the business judgment rule or its equivalent in the jurisdiction concerned must be addressed. The deference afforded to the rule or presumption varies considerably from jurisdiction to jurisdiction.[8]

In all jurisdictions and in all situations—including insolvency—the duty of directors is to manage the affairs of the corporation to maximize its value for the benefit of its stakeholders. When a corporation is solvent, those stakeholders are the corporation's shareholders. When the corporation is insolvent, the creditors take the place of the shareholders as the residual beneficiaries of any increase in its value. The insolvency representative, who replaces the directors of the company, is thus under a duty to maximize the assets of the corporation for the benefit of its creditors.[9]

In considering a cause of action against the directors or officers of a corporation, an insolvency representative would address both the mechanics of such an action and the likelihood of recovery. Even a strong cause of action is meaningless if the defendant has no assets against which to execute judgment. An insolvency representative will pursue only those claims for which investigation shows there are assets available to satisfy them. In other cases, an insolvency representative may consider pursuing other actors who facilitated breaches of duty or who may have received benefits. Banks, accounting, or audit firms that may have failed to discover fraud or dishonesty on the part of the directors of a company will likely have more assets than a director or officer who has fled the jurisdiction or who is insolvent. In some instances, directors' and officers' liability insurance may provide a recovery if a director has committed misconduct.

Corporate officers and directors are not permitted to use their position of trust and confidence to further their private interests. Any secret commissions received are recoverable by the company or, in the case of insolvency, by the insolvency representative. If a director had a personal financial interest in a transaction or received a benefit over and above that which flows to the corporation or all stockholders generally, that benefit is recoverable and the business judgment rule will not protect the decision to engage in it.

An insolvency representative must consider the applicable law in the jurisdiction of domicile of the corporation in determining whether to pursue an action against a director. Both procedural and substantive laws must be addressed, including laws on how to prove bad faith or on the presumption that operates in favor of the director. The fiduciary duties of directors in the jurisdiction must be analyzed as well as the liability standard for breaching them. An insolvency representative will need to ascertain whether a country's corporate governance jurisprudence prohibits directors from self-dealing and permits insolvency representatives to pursue actions to hold directors accountable for breaches of their fiduciary duties.

The World Bank Principles set out best practices for directors' obligations as well as possible liability and remedies for breach. When insolvency systems impose specific duties on directors, and they are regularly held accountable in practice, directors' incentives for malfeasance are reduced. In some jurisdictions, a bribe taker can be held accountable if he had a fiduciary duty, which can be relevant in the context of stolen asset cases. Box 3.4 sets out the World Bank Principle that addresses directors' obligation prior to insolvency.

BOX 3.4 | **World Bank Principle B2—Directors' Obligations in the Period Approaching Insolvency**

Laws governing directors' obligations in the period approaching insolvency should promote responsible corporate behavior while fostering reasonable risk taking and encouraging business reorganization. The law should provide appropriate remedies for breach of directors' obligations, which may be enforced after insolvency proceedings have commenced.

B2.1 The obligation. The law should require that when they know or reasonably ought to know that insolvency of the enterprise is imminent or unavoidable, directors should have due regard to the interests of creditors and other stakeholders, and should take reasonable steps to either avoid insolvency, or where insolvency is unavoidable, minimize its extent.

B2.2 Persons owing the obligation. The law should specify the persons owing the obligation, which may include any person formally appointed as a director and any other person exercising factual control and performing the functions of a director.

B2.3 Liability and remedies. Where creditors suffer loss or damage due to a director's breach of their obligations, the law should impose liability subject to possible defenses (including that the director took reasonable steps to avoid or minimize the extent of insolvency). The extent of any liability should not exceed the loss or damage suffered by creditors as a result of the breach. The law should specify that the remedies for liability found by the court to arise from a breach of the obligations should include payment in full to the insolvency estate of any damages assessed by the court. The insolvency representative should have primary standing to pursue a cause of action for breach.

B2.4 Funding of actions. The law should provide for the costs of an action against a director to be paid as administrative expenses.

Personal Liability Actions against Directors

In jurisdictions with well-developed insolvency frameworks, directors of insolvent companies may be held personally responsible, without any limitation of liability, for any or all of the debts or other liabilities of the company if they knowingly participated in the fraudulent operation of the businesses. These claims generally arise under "wrongful trading" or "duty to file" provisions when the company continues to operate and incur debts with, to the knowledge of the directors, no reasonable prospect of the creditors being paid. Directors can be personally liable for such debts.

Insolvency representatives have to demonstrate fault, damages, and causation as in typical tort cases. In some countries, it is sufficient to show that the action of the directors "contributed to the bankruptcy" to obtain compensation for the insufficiency of assets. In addition to fraud and criminal offenses, fault can include obvious managerial mistakes or dishonest actions, including risky investments, conduct of operations outside the company's purpose, lack of supervision, continuation of operations in spite of deficits, recourse to ruinous means to finance operations, or pursuit of activity in a personal interest.

In some countries, such as Belgium and France, the law allows actions against both legal and de facto directors who had the power to make managerial decisions. Directors or managers include those serving as of the commencement of insolvency proceedings and former directors. Former directors are liable only if the insufficiency of assets existed at the date of their resignation or removal and if the insufficiency was the result of their fraudulent activities. They may be obligated to pay compensation only for the increase in the shortfall of assets between the date on which they committed a fault and the final balance. In such countries, actions are generally time limited.[10]

Proceedings for Fraudulent or Wrongful Trading

Insolvency representatives who suspect wrongdoing on the part of directors may consider whether to pursue actions for fraudulent or wrongful trading—fraudulent trades can be used to justify payments to third parties or receive or conceal corrupt assets. The distinction between wrongful and fraudulent trading derives from the intent of the director. Wrongful trading involves mismanagement and might include, for example, failing to pay company tax liabilities or to file statutory returns. Fraudulent trading involves a deliberate attempt to defraud—dishonest intent can be inferred when, for example, a company continues trading even though the directors know that the company can no longer satisfy its current liabilities or when the directors cause the company to incur additional debt when they knew that there is no reasonable prospect of that debt being paid. In the United Kingdom, fraudulent and wrongful trading claims can now be assigned to third parties. Unsecured creditors, either individually or as a group, may pursue claims against directors.

The burden of proving fraudulent intent is high, which means that in practice the claim is rarely brought. One of the benefits of a fraudulent trading action in the United Kingdom, however, is that section 213 of the Insolvency Act 1986 has extraterritorial effect.[11] Section 213(2) provides:

> The court, on the application of the insolvency representative may declare that any persons who were knowingly parties to the carrying on of the business in the manner above-mentioned are to be liable to make such contributions (if any) to the company's assets as the court thinks proper.[12]

In the United Kingdom, an insolvency representative bringing a claim for wrongful trading need not show that the directors had knowledge or ought to have concluded that there was no reasonable prospect that the company would avoid insolvent liquidation at a specific time, only that they knew or ought to have known that the company had no reasonable prospect of avoiding liquidation *at some time* before the winding up. Once it has been established that a director knew or ought to have known that there was no reasonable prospect of the company avoiding liquidation, the onus of establishing a defense under section 214(3) of the Insolvency Act 1986 falls on the director. Directors must show that they made every effort to minimize the potential loss to the company's creditors.[13]

Section 213 of the Insolvency Act 1986 provides that if, during a company's winding up, it appears that any business has been carried on with intent of defrauding the company's creditors or the creditors of any other person, or for any fraudulent purpose, the court may, on the insolvency representative's application, declare that anyone who knowingly carried on the business is liable to make such contributions (if any) to the company's assets as the court thinks proper. Under section 214 of the Insolvency Act 1986, directors of a company in liquidation can be ordered by the court to contribute personally to the assets in the liquidation if they are found to have been guilty of wrongful trading. Claims for wrongful trading cannot be brought against nondirectors.

Preferences and Transactions at Undervalue

The ability to assign claims also applies to preferences[14] and transactions at undervalue. Preferential payments to a particular creditor, or the sale assets below their fair market value, are both likely to be investigated if a company becomes insolvent. Undervalued transactions in particular can be a way to shift "value" from one company to another—a method of laundering assets—which can be used by corrupt officials hiding funds.

An insolvency representative has a duty to investigate preferential payments and transactions at undervalue and can apply to the court to set them aside. In the United Kingdom, transactions at undervalue and preferences can be set aside pursuant to sections 238 and 239 of the Insolvency Act 1986, respectively. Similar provisions are found in most, if not all, jurisdictions with a codified insolvency framework. They differ with respect to the timeframe during which the transactions are subject to being set aside. In the United Kingdom, for example, transactions at undervalue within two years prior to the onset of insolvency are likely to be set aside. An insolvency representative may investigate potential preferences to a connected party going back two years and to a nonconnected party going back six months. There may also be differences between jurisdictions on the meaning of "onset of insolvency." The onset of insolvency is generally considered to be the date on which a petition or other document is filed initiating the process.

Other Breaches of Duty

Directors may be also held to account for other breaches of duty, such as, in the United Kingdom for example, the duty to avoid conflicts of interest; the duty to exercise reasonable care, skill, and diligence; the duty to act within lawful authority; the duty not to accept benefits from third parties; and the duty to declare one's interest in proposed transactions or arrangements.

Directors are also subject to other statutory requirements, such as the duty to keep proper books and records, and restrictions on entering into certain transactions with, or accepting loans from, the company. Breach of these duties and requirements can result not only in directors being disqualified from their positions but can also expose them to personal liability. The insolvency representative may bring such claims, and in some cases the directors may also be held criminally liable.

If property of the company has been misapplied or improperly retained, creditors, shareholders, or in the case of insolvency, the insolvency representative, can pursue claims against officers or others concerned in its management. Such claims can also be brought against facilitators. Potential causes of action that can be brought against officers or facilitators outside the statutory setting include actions for monies had and received, for unjust enrichment, and for knowing assistance or knowing receipt.

Actions commenced prior to insolvency by creditors or shareholders are often transferred to, and thereafter prosecuted by, the insolvency representative. If there are insufficient funds with which to pursue these actions (either by the insolvency representative or private parties), some jurisdictions permit their assignment to others who are financially able to prosecute them. Assignment provides an insolvency representative with funds that can be used either to pay creditors or to fund or partially fund other projects designed to maximize value for the estate. In the United Kingdom and the United States, the insolvency representative can also assign statutory causes of action. Fraudulent and wrongful trading claims can also be assigned to third parties, as can claims regarding preferences and transactions at undervalue. Assignment is not universally available, and, in common law jurisdictions, the laws of maintenance and champerty[15] may bar assignment or render it a nullity. Not all jurisdictions have repealed, or introduced the requisite exceptions to, the rules prohibiting the assignment or funding of certain causes of action.

In many civil law countries, insolvency laws contemplate a duty, mainly but not only on the part of management, to file for insolvency within a specified time after a director knows or should have known that the company would be unable to repay its debts. For example, Germany's insolvency statute (*Insolvenzordnung*) requires filing for insolvency within 21 days after a director acquires or should have acquired such knowledge. This has inspired many other similar laws, for example in the Balkans, that replicate or approximate the 21-day timeframe. In such jurisdictions, directors that do not file for insolvency within the specified period may be held liable.

Derivative Actions

What can be done if directors remain in charge of a company and they all agree to preserve the status quo? There is no prospect of an action being brought against delinquent officers. Assume that a shareholder, or group of shareholders, discovers that the company has been involved in a long-running corruption scheme, through which the directors have been receiving substantial kickbacks. The company is not insolvent, but the shareholders fear for the company's future.

Derivative actions, actions brought by shareholders, not to enforce their own rights, but to enforce the rights and liabilities of the company, are an especially useful tool when a company is controlled by "wrongdoers." A successful public prosecution does not guarantee recompense to shareholders who suffer financial loss; imposition of fines against the company may result in depleting the company's value even further. Private derivative actions enable shareholders to hold company management accountable for misconduct. Derivative actions can also be brought against advisers, such as auditing companies, who turned a blind eye to or actively facilitated corruption or mismanagement. In *WGI Emerging Markets Fund, LLC v. Petróleo Brasileiro S.A.*,[16] a derivative claim was filed in a federal court in New York against Petróleo Brasileiro S.A. (Petrobras) and PricewaterhouseCoopers (PwC) Auditores Independentes, accusing Petrobras of a "pervasive bribery and money laundering scheme," ignored by auditor PwC, that overstated the value of the company's assets and profitability by at least $17 billion. The case is still pending.

Piercing the Corporate Veil

Insolvency representatives may be faced with complex corporate structures in their attempt to recover value for an estate. A bankrupt or insolvent company may have transferred assets to a corporate entity in an attempt to evade liability or to frustrate the insolvency representative's efforts to recover or maximize value. Because a corporation has an independent identity, it can be difficult to reach the individuals behind the façade. By "piercing the corporate veil," the rights and duties of a corporation are considered to be the rights and liabilities of its shareholders. The English judiciary and others take a cautious approach to treating a company and its owners as the same legal entity, as shown in the recent decision of the English Supreme Court in *Prest v. Petrodel Resources Ltd.*[17] In *Prest*, a divorcing husband disputed his wife's right to share in properties owned in the name of corporations through which he had the right to transfer property. The Supreme Court upheld the principle set out in *Salomon v. Salomon*,[18] holding that the "corporate veil" should be pierced only in very limited circumstances. Lord Sumption, delivering the leading speech, referred to the limited exceptions as the "concealment principle" and the "evasion principle"[19] and emphasized the importance of the concept of separate corporate personality: "The separate personality and property of a company is sometimes described as a fiction, and in a sense, it is, but the fiction forms the whole foundation to English company and insolvency law."[20]

The courts will come to the aid of insolvency representatives or others, however, on a showing of evidence of deceit or an intention to evade legal obligation. In *Prest*, the Supreme Court did not leave the wife without remedy, holding instead that her husband held the property in the form of a resulting trust and that she was entitled to a portion of those properties (see box 3.5).

Following *Prest*, the corporate veil can be pierced only if a person seeks deliberately to evade a legal obligation, liability, or restriction by interposing a company under his control. In *Prest*, Lord Sumption limited the circumstances in which the separate corporate personality may be ignored to those involving evasion. In those circumstances, the Court may depart from the fundamental principle that a company is a legal personality separate from that of its owners and pierce the corporate veil, but only for the purpose of

---

BOX 3.5   *Prest v. Petrodel Resources Ltd.*[a]

Prest had set up and funded a number of companies to purchase real estate. In divorce proceedings in the United Kingdom, Justice Moylan ordered the transfer of seven U.K. properties, legally owned by British companies that Prest controlled, to Prest's ex-wife in partial satisfaction of a lump sum order on the grounds that Prest had effective control of the companies and was in the same position as if he had been the beneficiary of a bare trust or if the companies were his nominees.[b] The companies that owned the properties had existed for a number of years and, in some cases, had owned the properties before Prest's marriage. There was no suggestion that the companies had been set up to avoid legal obligations or that the companies were being run dishonestly. The companies appealed and won, and Prest's ex-wife appealed to the Supreme Court.

In the Supreme Court, Lord Sumption refused to pierce the corporate veil because the companies did not represent an attempt to hide assets. There was no evidence that the companies were deliberately set up to evade an obligation or frustrate the operation of law, in his view, the occasions when the veil should be pierced. Lord Sumption decided, however, that the properties owned by the companies were owned beneficially by Prest by means of a resulting trust, rather than by piercing the corporate veil. Under certain circumstances a transfer may not be deemed final and, despite the transferee's apparent ownership of the asset, the ownership "springs back" to the transferor. Vice Chancellor Megarry stated, in *Re Sick and Funeral Society of St John's Sunday School, Golcar*,[c] that a "resulting trust is essentially a property concept; any property that a man does not effectually dispose of remains his own."

a. [2013] UK SC 34.
b. Ibid., 39.
c. [1972] 2 All ER 439.

depriving the company or its controller of the advantage they would have obtained through the company's separate legal status. Lord Sumption referred to two principles:

> They can conveniently be called the concealment principle and the evasion principle. The concealment principle . . . does not involve piercing the corporate veil at all. . . . In these cases the court is not disregarding the "façade," but only looking behind it to discover the facts which the corporate structure is concealing. . . .
>
> The evasion principle is different. It is that the court may disregard the corporate veil if there is a legal right against the person in control of it which exists independently of the company's involvement, and a company is interposed so that the separate legal personality of the company will defeat the right or frustrate its enforcement.[21]

In *Wood v. Baker*, a court was willing to pierce the corporate veil in a bankruptcy.[22] The English High Court was willing to grant an injunction to the bankruptcy trustees and to pierce the corporate veil of companies that were operated by a bankrupt person as his agents and nominees and that held assets on his behalf (see box 3.6).

The theory of piercing the corporate veil can be applied in civil law jurisdictions. Judges may apply the legal concept of "confusion of estates" to refuse to differentiate between

---

BOX 3.6   *Wood v. Baker*[a]

Baker was declared bankrupt in 2005. He had been convicted and sentenced on multiple charges, including passport and invoice fraud and attempts to pervert the course of justice. His assets were held by third parties, including companies and other businesses. He had failed to cooperate with the trustees in bankruptcy, and his discharge from bankruptcy was suspended indefinitely.

Upon bankruptcy, all assets beneficially owned by a debtor vest in the trustees in bankruptcy pursuant to section 306 of the Insolvency Act 1986. Under section 307, if the bankrupt acquires other property during his bankruptcy (after-acquired property), the trustees can serve a written notice claiming the after-acquired property for the bankrupt's estate. Pursuant to section 307(3), ownership of such property is deemed to have vested in the trustees as of the date the debtor acquired his interest in it.

Following investigations into Baker's affairs, the trustees discovered that substantial sums of money were being paid through accounts held by certain companies. The trustees made an urgent application for an injunction to preserve the funds in those companies' bank accounts and sought declarations that the business and assets of the companies were held in trust for Baker and constituted after-acquired property.

The court granted the injunction against the companies, finding that there was evidence that Baker was effectively behind the various companies that were being used to shelter money, business, and assets that belonged to him and that the assets were subject to section 307(3).

a. [2015] EWHC 2536 (Ch).

---

what belongs to a shareholder or director of a company and what belongs to the corporate person. Judges may apply the same concept to companies whose equity is held by a parent company. As a result, a parent company, shareholders, or directors can be held liable for the debt of the insolvent entity. Boxes 3.7, 3.8, and 3.9 illustrate how this approach is applied in Brazil.

BOX 3.7 *Bankruptcy Estate of Petroforte v. Securinvest Holdings S.A.*

In *Bankruptcy Estate of Petroforte v. Securinvest Holdings S.A.*, the trustee of Petroforte filed a request in civil court to pierce the corporate veil and to extend the bankruptcy to another economic group (Securinvest Group), arguing that both economic groups acted as one in order to divert assets from Petroforte, in prejudice of the creditors of the Petroforte Bankruptcy Estate. The debts of the Petroforte Bankruptcy Estate were estimated to be approximately $400 million.

The final ruling on the merits was issued by Minister Nancy Andrighi of the Superior Court of Justice, the highest Brazilian federal court, affirming the piercing of the corporate veil and the extension of the bankruptcy to approximately $300 million of assets owned by Securinvest Group, including an ethanol plant, farms, real estate, a hotel, and other assets. *Petroforte* set the national precedent for piercing the corporate veil and establishing a preponderance of the evidence as the standard of proof. The case shows that economic crimes, which are always evolving, require contemporary and innovative solutions, including disregarding the legal entity when the entity has no real independence from parent companies or stakeholders.

BOX 3.8 *Bankruptcy Estate of Mabe Brasil v. Mabe/General Electric/ Penteado Family[a]*

BSH Continental (BSH) was a major appliance manufacturer with headquarters in São Paulo State. In 2009, BSH was acquired by the Mexican group Mabe, and renamed Mabe Brasil. The Penteado family and General Electric (GE) also invested in Mabe Brasil, acquiring part of its stock. Shortly after their investment, the Penteados and GE filed for judicial reorganization of Mabe Brasil and, in February 2016, Mabe Brasil was declared bankrupt. More than 2,000 employees were unpaid and left unemployed. Data collection and forensic work performed by the bankruptcy trustee showed that the controllers of Mabe Brasil drained its assets, leading to the insolvency.

Based on the findings of fraud, the trustee applied to pierce the corporate veil, requesting an ex parte freeze order against Mabe Brasil's former controllers. The State Court noted that even before the company entered judicial reorganization, Mabe Brasil, with the knowledge and participation of the Penteado Family, the GE Group, and Mabe México, conducted improper and predatory actions that depleted the company's assets and ultimately led to its insolvency.

(continued next page)

Bankruptcy Estate of Mabe Brasil v. Mabe/General Electric/ Penteado Family (continued)

The State Court argued that the right invoked by the plaintiff was plausible and the grant of a preliminary freeze order was justified, not only because the respondents were freely able to travel abroad, but because the shifts in shareholder control of the respondent companies might prevent the identification of their beneficial owners and the whereabouts of their assets.

An ex parte order was issued, freezing US$266 million in the respondents' accounts. The judge, taking into account the need for secrecy, ordered that the freeze be kept under seal during this process, enhancing its effectiveness. The seal would be lifted after the orders were carried out.

GE was the first respondent to file an interlocutory appeal, requesting a suspension of the order. After the São Paulo Court of Appeal denied the motion for a suspension, GE filed a writ of mandamus, which was terminated by Court of Appeal Judge Cesar Ciampolini with the following remark: "Extreme situations deserve from the judiciary, once it is provoked, proportional and reasonable measures, which can be drastic, in order to preserve the right of individuals in good faith, preserving the useful result of legal actions tackling fraud."[b]

a. State of São Paulo, No. 1000641-02.2019.8.26.0229, Mabe Brasil Eletrodomésticos LTDA, General Electric International (Benelux) B.V.
b. Ibid.

MMX Sudeste under reorganization v. Batista[a]

MMX Sudeste, based in Belo Horizonte, State of Minas Gerais, Brazil, is directly owned by EBX Economic Group, and ultimately owned by Eike Fuhrken Batista da Silva. Batista has in the past been listed as one of the richest men in the world. MMX Sudeste's core business is extraction and trade of iron and minerals, and it holds extraction rights for mines in the middle eastern section of Brazil. It filed for judicial reorganization on October 16, 2014.

The judicial administrator appointed by the court suspected that MMX Sudeste became insolvent due to fraud, including fraudulent accounting that misled investors and the market. An investigation was authorized by the court to determine whether the shareholders and the controlling minds of MMX Sudeste should be held liable for its debts. Data collection showed that Batista, using MMX Sudeste, lured investors worldwide, advertising results that he knew the company was unable to produce, using a modus operandi similar to that perpetrated by other companies of EBX Economic Group.

Based on findings of fraud, an order was issued in 2017 to pierce the corporate veil to reach the controllers of MMX Sudeste. The order created an important precedent in Brazil because it was issued even though a plan of payments was

(continued next page)

BOX 3.9   *MMX Sudeste under reorganization v. Batista (continued)*

approved by the creditors. For the Brazilian court, the creditors' approval of the plan of payments was not an impediment to recovering the money.

Data collected in an auxiliary insolvency proceeding in the United States showed a flow of money from MMX Sudeste to several other offshore entities and to Batista's older son, who had acted as Batista's strawman, incorporating entities, hiring lawyers, and paying bills. A second order was issued in Brazil in March 2019 by Honorable Judge Claudia Helena Batista (no relation), piercing the corporate veil to reach the offshore entities and Batista's son and to hold them liable for MMX Sudeste's debts.

a. State of Minas Gerais, No. 19.006.144-0, MMX Sudeste under Reorganization v. Batista.

Key Points from this Chapter

- Although the UNCAC is explicit about the need to criminalize both bribe payers and receivers, many legislative provisions focus on the bribe payer.

- Insolvency proceedings can be useful for prosecuting bribe payers, particularly when intermediaries are involved and can be placed into liquidation. Pursuing bribe takers through insolvency proceedings is challenging but possible in certain jurisdictions.

- Agents or facilitators (such as lawyers, accountants, banks, or other intermediaries) whose identity can be discovered, either through an insolvency representative's statutory powers of investigation or through an application for a *Norwich Pharmacal* order, can also be targeted in insolvency proceedings.

- Maximizing value in winding-up cases can entail the monetization of intangibles, including potential claims for damages against persons who have diminished or enabled harm against the debtor's estate.

- Substantial value can potentially be recovered from damages claims directed against third-party facilitators and agents who have enabled the perpetration of acts of public corruption.

- The "duty of care" generally requires that directors and managers exercise the degree of care that ordinarily careful and prudent people would use under the circumstances.

- In some jurisdictions, a director may be held personally responsible for all debts or liabilities of an insolvent company if he was knowingly a party to fraud.

- Insolvency representatives may pursue actions for preferences, transactions at undervalue, breach of duty, or fraudulent or wrongful trading.

- Derivative actions (brought by shareholders to enforce the rights of the company) are a useful tool if a company is controlled by "wrongdoers."

- Piercing the corporate veil is the legal decision to treat the rights and duties of a corporation as the rights and liabilities of its shareholders.

Notes

1. In financial regulation, PEP describes someone who has been entrusted with a prominent public function. PEPs generally present a higher risk for potential involvement in bribery and corruption by virtue of their position and influence.
2. Transparency International UK, "London Property: Top Destination for Money Launderers" (December 1, 2016), https://www.transparency.org.uk/publications/london-property-tr-ti-uk/.
3. The United Kingdom makes an exception to this rule when the bribe taker has committed offenses under section 2 of the Bribery Act and if there are territorial links under section 12.
4. The assets were tied to 1Malaysia Development Berhad, which was established as a strategic development company under the Malaysia Ministry of Finance.
5. A full discussion of what constitutes a divergent and often confusing body of law in this area and across jurisdictions is beyond the scope of this publication.
6. [2003] UKHL 49.
7. Ibid., para. 77.
8. In Germany, for example, courts accord a lesser degree of deference to corporate decision makers in exercising their business judgment than would the courts of Delaware in the United States. There is no explicit statutory business judgment rule in French corporate law. French courts are unlikely, however, to second guess business decisions as long as the corporation remains solvent and the actions are within the limits defined by the laws and the stated purpose of the company. Within the EU, Croatia, Germany, Greece, Portugal, Romania, and Spain have codified a version of the business judgment rule. Austria, Belgium, Bulgaria, Cyprus, Denmark, Finland, Hungary, Italy, Lithuania, Luxembourg, Slovenia, Sweden, and the United Kingdom have no express rule but in practice afford some margin of discretion for directors in making business decisions. The Czech Republic, Estonia, France, Ireland, Latvia, Malta, Poland, and the Slovak Republic have neither an express nor implied business judgment rule. (Gerner-Beuerle et al. 2013).
9. In some jurisdictions, the debtor remains "in possession" after initiation of the insolvency process, either administering the assets itself (as in the United States, for example) or co-administering them under the supervision of the insolvency representative. In these cases, the debtor would owe a fiduciary duty to the residual beneficiaries, the creditors.
10. In France, an action must be instituted in the commercial court within three years after the liquidation judgment. The action is usually initiated by the insolvency representative, but article L651-3 of the Commercial Code also authorizes the public prosecutor to do so.
11. Jetivia SA v. Bilta (UK) Ltd. [2015] UKSC 23. In this case, which was brought by a liquidator, the defendant argued that the company itself was a wrongdoer and therefore could not sue directors for breach of fiduciary duty under the doctrine of illegality. The argument was rejected.
12. Insolvency Act 1986, § 213(2).
13. See Brooks and Willetts v. Armstrong and Walker [2015] EWHC 2289 (CH).

14. A preference is any transaction that puts a creditor, or any surety or guarantor of the company's liabilities, in a position better than that they would have upon liquidation or administration.
15. Maintenance and champerty, often considered antiquated, are doctrines in common law jurisdictions to preclude frivolous litigation. "Maintenance" occurs when a disinterested party encourages the bringing of a lawsuit. "Champerty" is the financial support of a party to a lawsuit in return for a share of the recovery. Champerty, where legal, is now commonly known as litigation financing, and the agreements are most often made with third-party funders.
16. WGI Emerging Markets Fund, LLC v. Petróleo Brasileiro S.A. (Petrobras) (In re Petrobras Securities Universities Superannuation Scheme Ltd.), Docket No. 16-1914-cv (2d Cir. July 7, 2017).
17. [2013] UKSC 34.
18. [1897] AC 22.
19. [2013] UKSC 34, 28.
20. Ibid., 8.
21. Prest v. Petrodel Resources Ltd. [2013] UKSC 34.
22. [2015] EWHC 2536 (Ch).

References

Gerner-Beuerle, Carsten, Philipp Paech, and Edmund Philipp Schuster. 2013. *Study on Directors' Duties and Liability*. London: LSE Enterprise.

McLachlan, Tom, and Dafni Loizou. 2017. "Jurisdiction of the English Court to Wind Up Foreign Companies in the Public Interest." Charles Russell Speechlys. https://www.charlesrussellspeechlys.com/en/news-and-insights/insights/litigation--dispute-resolution/2017/jurisdiction-of-the-english-court-to-wind-up-foreign-companies-in-the-public-interest/.

OECD (Organisation for Economic Co-operation and Development). 2009. *Working Group on Bribery Annual Report*. Paris: OECD.

Clients who consult lawyers are entitled to the protection of legal professional or attorney-client privilege: their communications are confidential and unavailable to third parties. The usefulness of these communications to an insolvency representative seeking targets and sources of information raises the question of when the privilege applies. The ability of an insolvency representative to access privileged material can change the course of a case of corruption or asset tracing. In *Federal Republic of Brazil and Municipality of São Paulo v. Durant International Ltd. and Kildare Finance Ltd.*,[1] discussed in box I.1, the first documents obtained by the court-appointed insolvency representatives of the defendant companies came from the lawyers who had acted for the companies at trial—documents that were covered by privilege. Because the insolvency representatives were appointed to control the companies, however, they were entitled to documents in the company's possession. The information proved to be tremendously helpful.

This chapter provides an overview of the core principles of privilege in the common law jurisdictions of the United Kingdom and the United States and the civil law jurisdiction of France, including the extent of the privilege and who has the right to assert it. The chapter considers how the normal rules of privilege can be modified for different insolvency processes and, in particular, whether privilege belongs to the insolvent body or individual or to the insolvency representative, and how the answer to this question—which can vary according to the type of insolvency procedure—may affect the representative's ability to waive privilege and access probative evidence. In asset recovery proceedings, for example, the claimant may be able to gain access to information previously shared with the corrupt entity's lawyer if ownership of the privileged material is deemed to vest in the claimant.

Privilege in England

Forms of Privilege at Common Law

Privilege is a fundamental legal right. It allows parties to litigation, arbitration, and investigations to resist disclosure of confidential and sensitive material. This section discusses two types of privilege under U.K. law—legal advice privilege and litigation privilege. The English rules on privilege have generally been adopted in other Commonwealth jurisdictions, including Guernsey, the Isle of Man, and Jersey.

Legal Advice Privilege

Legal advice privilege protects confidential communications, whether written or oral, between lawyers and clients, made for the purpose of giving or receiving legal advice.

The privilege protects the communications of both lawyers and clients. The privilege ensures that, in the interests of justice, parties can seek advice openly from lawyers, without fear that what is said may be repeated to another party or stated in court. It enables clients to be fully transparent in discussing their affairs with legal advisers. The privilege extends even to lawyers' preparatory materials that are not communicated to clients. Although communications between lawyers and clients must be confidential, not all confidential and sensitive material is privileged. Privilege applies only to documents that are both confidential and not publicly available. It covers advice given in a legal context, but would not, for example, cover situations in which lawyers act in a business, executive, or administrative capacity. This caveat predominantly affects in-house lawyers who may perform general business functions in addition to their legal roles.

The term "lawyer" encompasses a foreign qualified lawyer, a barrister or solicitor, a paralegal or trainee (provided they are supervised by a qualified lawyer) and, generally, an in-house lawyer. It does not, however, extend to other professions, such as accountants, even when they provide advice on, for example, tax law. The European Court of Justice has also held that communications between a company and its in-house lawyers during a competition investigation are not protected by legal advice privilege because in-house lawyers, unlike outside counsel, are not considered sufficiently independent. The definition of client has been restricted under recent English case law[2] to refer, for a corporate entity, only to those individuals who have been instructed to obtain legal advice on a matter rather than to all employees.

Litigation Privilege

Litigation privilege protects a wider category of documents—those between clients or lawyers and third parties—but only when they are created (1) after proceedings have been commenced or contemplated, and (2) for the dominant purpose of seeking or giving advice in such proceedings.

Because litigation privilege can potentially protect a wide class of documents, the courts carefully analyze whether the two criteria have been met. Litigation privilege applies only when litigation or arbitration has already begun or is genuinely contemplated. If a communication has more than one purpose, a court will assess its purpose objectively, taking into account all the relevant circumstances. Recent case law has sought to limit the scope of the litigation privilege, suggesting that documents created to obtain advice about how to avoid anticipated litigation are not privileged and reasserting that documents whose primary purpose is to investigate whether wrongdoing has occurred are not privileged.[3]

Common Interest Privilege

Clients with joint or common interests may share privilege of communications; each party will be entitled to assert the privilege against third parties. This right will remain after any breakdown of their relationship, such as the case of a divorcing couple.

Which Law Applies?

Notwithstanding that privilege is generally considered a substantive right,[4] English courts apply the law of the forum for the purpose of privilege, that is, English law in any dispute in an English court, irrespective of the law that governs the substantive dispute.

What is the result when the question of whether documents are privileged is governed by, for example, Luxembourg law, but the insolvency proceeding is being heard in England? *Re Hellas Telecommunications (Luxembourg) II SCA*[5] provides the answer. The insolvency representative argued that the issue of which law applies was governed by the European Commission Regulation on Insolvency Proceedings 1346/2000 (the precursor to European Union (EU) Regulation 2015/848). England has substantive jurisdiction over all liquidations taking place in its courts.

The respondent argued that the insolvency representative's right to receive the information and documentation was governed by Luxembourg law. The English court should not exercise its discretionary powers under section 236 of the Insolvency Act 1986 (Insolvency Act) to order the inspection of documents because the disclosure would breach Luxembourg's laws of professional secrecy.

The court ruled that the applicable law was English. Insolvency proceedings are governed by the law of the Member State in which they were commenced.[6] "Main insolvency proceedings"[7] had been opened in England, and there were no secondary proceedings elsewhere; therefore English law applied.

Luxembourg law, under which the legal advice had been sought, would be relevant to the exercise of the English court's discretion. Any order made by the English court could be recognized by a Luxembourg court under article 25 of the Regulation, and that court could decide whether the English order violated the public policy of Luxembourg under article 26 of the Regulation.

Waiver

Privilege is an absolute right, and courts do not engage in a balancing test to determine whether a legitimate claim to privilege can be denied. The person to whom the privilege belongs may choose to waive it. A litigant in possession of a favorable legal opinion with respect to its claim may choose to show it to the other side to facilitate settlement.

Insolvency

It is important in an insolvency to determine to whom privilege belongs. Can an insolvent entity assert privilege over legal advice provided prior to the insolvency, or does the privilege vest in the insolvency representative, who can choose to waive it? The answer to the question can affect an insolvency representative's ability to use his ancillary powers, discussed in chapter 2, such as voiding transactions at undervalue or transactions defrauding creditors. Insolvent entities often take legal advice on ways to keep assets out of creditors' reach; uncovering such advice can help determine whether assets were legally or fraudulently transferred. English law varies according to whether the insolvent is an individual or a corporate entity.

Individual Bankruptcy

An individual's ability to assert privilege in an insolvency has been clarified in two recent cases. In *Avonwick Holdings Ltd. v. Shlosberg*,[8] the Court of Appeal held that the privilege attaching to information and documents of a bankrupt person was not property that vested in the trustees under the Insolvency Act.

Shlosberg was a Russian businessman based in England. Shlosberg failed to pay a substantial judgment awarded to Avonwick and was bankrupted on Avonwick's petition. Avonwick was represented in the proceedings against Shlosberg by solicitors who were then appointed to act for Shlosberg's trustees in bankruptcy, a relatively common scenario. The trustees exercised their powers under section 311(1) of the Insolvency Act to obtain privileged and confidential documents held by Shlosberg's former solicitors. The trustees provided those documents to the solicitors who acted both for them and for Avonwick. Avonwick subsequently issued proceedings against Shlosberg for conspiracy, based in part on the privileged documents.

The trustees argued that the privilege was theirs and could be waived by them. They argued that they were entitled, as trustees, to take possession of the documents that contained the privileged information, and that the Insolvency Act provides that trustees can exercise any powers with respect to a bankrupt's property that the bankrupt himself could have exercised. They also cited case law that a trustee who obtains title to specific property of the bankrupt also obtains ancillary rights of privilege with respect to that property.

The Court of Appeal, however, held that privilege in English law is a fundamental right. Curtailing the right of privilege by statute requires express words or necessary implication. The court rejected the argument that rights of privilege constitute property within the meaning of the Insolvency Act. The trustees had also suggested that an abrogation of privilege was implicit in section 311(1) of the Insolvency Act. Section 311(1) provides that privilege does not entitle a bankrupt to refuse to supply documents relating to his estate to the trustee. The court held, however, that, although a trustee could use such documents in the bankruptcy, he had to preserve their privilege in doing so.

The Court of Appeal also held that, even if Shlosberg's privilege in the documents had been lost, providing the documents to an individual creditor to aid its litigation against the bankrupt person is not a purpose of bankruptcy.

The Court of Appeal left open the question whether a trustee in bankruptcy who takes possession of specific property to which legal advice relates inherits privilege with respect to that property. *Crescent Farm (Sidcup) Sports Ltd. v. Sterling Officers Ltd.*,[9] a decision of first instance, suggested that the benefit of the privilege would pass with the property, which became known as the *Crescent Farm* principle.

In a later bankruptcy proceeding, the High Court decided this question in favor of the bankrupt. In *Leeds v. Lemos*,[10] the trustee sought to give a creditor access to the bankrupt's privileged documents to enable the creditor to bring an action to set aside certain transactions entered into prior to the bankruptcy. The trustee relied on the *Crescent Farm* principle. The court ruled, however, that there should be no distinction between documents relating to bankruptcy assets and those relating to liabilities when considering the effect of the bankruptcy on privilege. *Crescent Farm* was distinguishable because that case did not involve bankruptcy. Privilege was a fundamental common law right, and the court had no authority to direct a bankrupt person to waive it under the Insolvency Act or otherwise. The court added that even if the *Crescent Farm* principle applied to the automatic vesting of property in a trustee in bankruptcy, any property recovered under a claim challenging transactions that predated the bankruptcy would not constitute "property" for the purposes of the Insolvency Act.

The two judgments together provide that there is no distinction between the privileges relating to asset and liability documents—a trustee has the right to see privileged information when necessary for the performance of his statutory function. There is, however, no authority in the Insolvency Act that allows a court to compel a bankrupt person to waive privilege.

Care should be taken when dealing with privileged documents. Although a trustee has the right to see privileged documents, which may prove helpful in carrying out his statutory function, and to use them in proceedings against the bankrupt person, the trustee can neither waive privilege without the bankrupt's consent, nor compel waiver by court order. In practice, a bankrupt person is unlikely to agree to waive privilege. Trustees should instruct solicitors different from those used by major creditors or, when one law firm acts for both, instruct a different group within the firm and establish a firewall.

Corporate Insolvency

Unlike in an individual bankruptcy, the property of a corporate bankrupt is not transferred to the trustee. Instead the insolvency representative takes control of the company, its assets and liabilities, and the benefit of any privileged legal advice the company has received.[11] The insolvency representative or administrator acts as an agent of the company and can waive the company's privilege.

This approach favors insolvency representatives and creditors. Public policy may also play a role—individuals have more rights than companies. Moreover, a company may not exist after insolvency. Nevertheless, allowing a trustee in bankruptcy to see privileged documents, but not to use them, even against the bankrupt individual, raises practical difficulties. The rules on privilege in the United States and France are described in the remainder of this chapter.

Privilege in the United States

U.S. laws on privilege broadly mirror the English rules. The purpose of privilege is to "encourage full and frank communication between attorneys and their clients and thereby promote broader public interests in the observance of law and administration of justice."[12]

To establish the privilege, a party must demonstrate that a communication between client and counsel (1) was intended to be and was kept confidential, and (2) was made for the purpose of obtaining or providing legal advice. The work product doctrine is similar to the English concept of litigation privilege.

Corporate Insolvency

In *Commodity Futures Trading Commission v. Weintraub*,[13] the U.S. Supreme Court held that, because the attorney-client privilege is controlled outside of bankruptcy by a corporation's management, the person or body whose duties most closely resemble those of management should control the privilege within bankruptcy.

In a corporate bankruptcy, the right to exercise attorney-client privilege passes to the trustee, including a liquidation trustee, provided the trustee has been vested with control over the debtor's bankrupt estate or the particular claims to which the privilege applies.

Personal Insolvency

The control of privilege in a consumer bankruptcy is more complex. As is true in English law, the rights of an individual differ significantly from those of a corporation. The Fifth Amendment's protection against self-incrimination is not available to a corporation. The case law governing the control of attorney-client privilege in individual bankruptcies varies between, and within, federal circuits.

In a liquidation under chapter 7 of the Bankruptcy Code, the trustee, rather than the individual debtor, controls the assets of the bankrupt estate. Which of them controls attorney-client privilege? Case law falls into three categories: (1) those that allow the trustee to control attorney-client privilege in individual bankruptcies; (2) those that give the individual debtor exclusive control over attorney-client privilege; and (3) those that balance the facts and circumstances to determine whether the individual debtor or the chapter 7 trustee controls the privilege. The most common approach is the balancing test.

Prospective claimants should determine which test the relevant jurisdiction follows if attorney-client privilege is likely to be an issue in a bankruptcy proceeding.

The law is now clear in the United Kingdom that bankrupt individuals have greater rights to preserve their privileged documents than insolvent corporations. This mirrors the U.S. position and may have its origins in the rights individuals have that corporations do not. Whatever party one represents, whether a corporation, individual, or trustee, a lawyer must carefully consider issues of privilege and their potential effects on the client.

Professional Secrecy in France

French law does not define legal privilege. The relationship between a lawyer and a client is protected, however, by the *secret professionnel* (professional secrecy).

The general principle is established in article 226-13 of the French Criminal Code. It applies to any professional in a position to receive confidential information, including administrators appointed by courts, and may also be imposed upon individuals by their professional codes.

Professional secrecy as applied to attorneys is established by article 2 of the *Code de Déontologie*, the attorneys' code of ethics. An attorney is a confidant of his client and therefore the information they exchange is protected by professional secrecy.

Scope and Application of the Professional Secret

The obligation of professional secrecy imposed on attorneys is general, absolute, and unlimited in time; it applies to all professional information and documents exchanged between clients and their attorneys during their professional relationship. Information given to attorneys through a personal relationship, however, is not protected.[14]

Professional secrecy covers not only information given to attorneys by clients, but also information relating to clients or their cases provided to attorneys by third parties, as well as any conclusion drawn by attorneys on the basis of the information received.

Sanctions for Violation of Professional Secrecy by an Attorney

Violations of professional secrecy can include giving protected information to a third party, such as a judge, another party to the litigation, the media, or a former client. Under article 226-13 of the French Criminal Code, a violation can subject an attorney to one year of imprisonment and a fine of up to €15,000.

An attorney who violates professional secrecy can also be sanctioned by the disciplinary board that regulates the legal profession.

Issues Relating to Corporate Insolvency and Bankruptcy Proceedings

In a corporate insolvency, the court will determine whether the insolvency representative will have access to documents and information held by the company's attorney or whether the attorney will be able to withhold the information under professional secrecy. The same issue arises with respect to information held by other professionals bound by professional secrecy such as banks, chartered accountants, and auditors.

The insolvency representative temporarily represents the company and takes over its management, which provides him with access to all information and documents, including information that would otherwise be subject to professional secrecy. The company's attorney will not be entitled to withhold that information.

Professionals who receive confidential information, such as company auditors, cannot invoke professional secrecy to withhold information from a bankruptcy judge or an insolvency representative. Professional secrecy does not apply even though the insolvency representative is a third party.

Although insolvency representatives have access to information and documents protected by professional secrecy, creditors of insolvent companies do not have access to documents protected by professional secrecy.

Issues Relating to Individual Insolvency

In individual insolvency proceedings, an insolvency representative's rights are limited to actions relating to the individual's professional activities. Under article L622-3 of the Commercial Code, the individual retains the right to manage his personal estate and make personal decisions.

There is no law on professional secrecy in individual insolvency proceedings or any law that entitles insolvency representatives to personal information that is subject to professional secrecy. An individual's lawyer may be able to invoke professional secrecy against an insolvency representative with respect to personal information given to him by the individual.

By analogy, a company attorney who has privileged and personal information about a director or officer of the company should be able to invoke professional secrecy against an insolvency representative with respect to matters that do not concern or prejudice the company; this, however, is only a hypothesis.

Conclusion

In France, an insolvent or bankrupt company has the right to invoke professional secrecy in dealing with third parties. Neither the company nor the attorney, however, will be able to invoke professional secrecy against an insolvency representative with respect to documents exchanged by the attorney and the company. The insolvency representative will be entitled to use these documents in litigation or asset recovery. Personal, nonprofessional information relating to a director or an officer may be entitled to confidentiality, although there is no case law on the issue.

Key Points from this Chapter

- In cases of corruption and asset tracing, the ability of insolvency representatives to access privileged material can change the course of a case.

- In English and Commonwealth systems, legal advice privilege protects confidential communications between a lawyer and her client for the purpose of giving or receiving legal advice. Litigation privilege protects a wider category of documents—those between a client or lawyer and a third party.

- In the U.S. and U.K. systems, a party claiming privilege must demonstrate that a communication between client and counsel was intended to be confidential and was made to obtain or provide legal advice.

- Bankrupt individuals have greater rights to preserve their privileged communications than insolvent corporations in the United Kingdom and the United States.

- In France, neither the company nor the attorney can invoke professional secrecy against an insolvency representative.

Notes

1. [2015] UKPC 35.
2. Three Rivers (No. 5) [2004] EWCA Civ. 218; the RBS Rights Issue Litigation [2016] EWCH 3161 (Ch).
3. [2017] EWHC 1017 (QB).
4. The RBS Rights Issue Litigation [2016] EWCH 3161 (Ch).
5. [2013] B.P.I.R. 756.
6. European Commission Regulation on Insolvency Proceedings 1346/2000, art. 4.
7. Ibid., art. 3.
8. [2016] EWCA Civ. 1138.
9. [1971] 3 All ER 1192.
10. [2017] EWHC 1825 (Ch).
11. Re Brook Martin [1993] BCLC 328.
12. Upjohn Co. v. United States, 449 U.S. 383 (1981).
13. 471 U.S. 343 (1985).
14. Cass. crim., 2 mars 2010, n°09-88.453.

5. Further Issues on the Use of Insolvency for Asset Recovery

Major Challenges for Asset Recovery in Developing Jurisdictions

Global insolvency systems vary around the world. In many developing countries, outdated insolvency laws remain on the books and there may be limited or no local experience in conducting insolvency cases. These jurisdictions may face challenges in using insolvency as a tool for cross-border asset recovery. This section discusses some of the challenges that may frustrate the efficient recovery of assets through insolvency proceedings in developing countries. Many of these challenges can be overcome; it is important, however, to be aware of them and to address them with a local lawyer experienced in insolvency proceedings. Some of the challenges discussed in this section apply to varying degrees in developed jurisdictions.

Jurisdiction matters significantly—in law and in practice—for both standard insolvency processes and the recovery of assets. If the matter is a corporate insolvency case filed against a company incorporated in an offshore jurisdiction, for example, the offshore law and jurisdiction would most likely apply. However, if a bribe-taking company is incorporated in a developing country, that country's law and jurisdiction would most likely apply.[1] Therefore, a claimant seeking asset recovery must be ready to face the challenges highlighted in this section of the guidebook.

Commencement Obstacles

Insolvency proceedings can be commenced if a debtor is unable to pay debts as they come due or if the debtor's balance sheet shows that liabilities exceed assets. Many developing jurisdictions, especially those using civil law systems, do not provide for the commencement of insolvency proceedings on just and equitable grounds, as do some common law jurisdictions. This presents a significant obstacle for asset recovery if the bribe-taking debtor is solvent.

Further, because of unclear legislation or lack of expertise, many developing countries do not have well-defined criteria for the commencement of insolvency cases. Even if the grounds for commencement would typically be sufficient elsewhere, a claimant (in this guidebook likely the state pursuing the recovery of assets) may have difficulty bringing a case in a developing jurisdiction.

Unregulated or Insufficiently Regulated Insolvency Representatives

Many of the suggestions in this guidebook presume that a jurisdiction has an established concept of "insolvency representative." Some developing countries, however, provide little or no guidance or regulation for insolvency representatives. Some countries specify categories of professionals (such as lawyers and accountants) that can be appointed as insolvency representatives without necessarily requiring that the individuals appointed have any specialized knowledge of insolvency. Others have regulations for insolvency representatives but lack a regulatory body to monitor them or respond to complaints. Others have remuneration systems with potentially skewed incentives: for example, the longer a case takes, the more the representative is paid. In many jurisdictions, creditors do not have a say in the appointment of the insolvency representative, and courts may be legally obligated to appoint, for example, a randomly selected individual; depending on the appointee's experience and knowledge, this approach might leave important features of a case unaddressed. In some jurisdictions, insolvency representatives have colluded with debtors, past management, or other parties. Comparing a jurisdiction's regulatory framework for insolvency representatives with the European Bank for Reconstruction and Development's Insolvency Office Holder Principles discussed in box 1.4 provides a basis for identifying the weaknesses in a jurisdiction's system.

Ineffective or Nonexistent Anti-Avoidance System

As discussed in the sections in chapter 3 titled *Proceedings for Fraudulent or Wrongful Trading* and *Preferences and Transactions at Undervalue*, in leading practice jurisdictions, voidable transactions and the look-back period enable insolvency representatives to cancel transactions that are improper or prejudicial. In other jurisdictions, however, (1) there may be no legal provision allowing the insolvency representative to cancel transactions (a small minority of countries, because avoidance actions have become standard); (2) laws that permit avoidance are unclear or incomplete; (3) look-back periods are too short; and (4) laws have procedural or design problems, such as the failure to specify that creditors can pursue avoidance actions if the insolvency representative fails to do so.

If a jurisdiction does not enable an insolvency representative to avoid improper transactions, or if the law is not sufficiently clear, fraudulent proceeds may be recoverable using the criminal law or other breach of duty regulations, such as the civil law "actio pauliana" (action to avoid fraud, analogous to recovering a fraudulent conveyance under common law).

Slow, Unresponsive, or Inexperienced Judicial Systems and Lawyers

Insolvency proceedings used for the recovery of stolen assets benefit from proceeding quickly. The longer a proceeding takes, the greater the risk that assets will be transferred, documents will disappear, or witnesses will move out of reach.

The World Bank's *Doing Business Report 2019* (2018) indicates that, in Latin America and the Caribbean and in Sub-Saharan Africa, almost three years pass, on average, between a company's default and the payment of some or all of the money owed to a creditor. The process takes a little over half that time in countries in the Organisation for Economic Co-operation and Development.[2] In some jurisdictions, recalcitrant debtors have many tactics at their disposal to delay proceedings. In jurisdictions where little or no action can take place until an appeal has been heard (especially appeals of interlocutory decisions), multiple appeals are often filed. The appellate process can take years to complete. In many countries there is no limit on the number of extensions of time or adjournments that can be granted.

Many developing countries have general courts that handle a wide range of issues from criminal to family to corporate law, making it difficult for judges to master complex and technical areas of law such as insolvency. This can slow down proceedings or lead to incorrect decisions. Only 101 of the 190 countries measured by the World Bank's *Doing Business Report 2019* (2018, 56) have specialized commercial courts, and only 31 have bankruptcy courts for insolvency cases. Specialized commercial or insolvency jurisdiction can result in shorter resolution times (World Bank 2018, 56). Training judges on insolvency is critical.

In some jurisdictions, the ability to bring cases in dedicated commercial courts or before dedicated insolvency judges may enable claimants to avoid these delays.

Ineffective or Nonexistent Collateral Registry Systems

A modern collateral registry system—centralized, notice-based, and accessible online—is another valuable component of the insolvency framework for asset recovery. Registries allow a lender to take a security interest in an asset without the requirement of physical custody. The debtor retains title and possession. Without registration of these transactions, there is no transparent guarantee for the lender and no assurance that the lender is the only one claiming an asset. When a debt is originated, collateral registries enable potential creditors or buyers to discover any existing liens on a property and allow them to register their own security interest, establishing priority over other creditors in case of the debtor's default. Collateral registries also enable insolvency representatives to quickly identify which assets are owned free and clear by the company and which have been used as collateral for lending. In asset recovery cases, the registry enables insolvency representatives to trace company assets and determine whether they are subject to liens. Insolvency representatives can also confirm which encumbered assets are subject to the collateral guarantee.

Many developing countries, however, do not have modern collateral registries. As of 2015, only 18 of 189 countries had a modern registry system. Only 25 countries had a notice-based registry, and 28 had an online registry (World Bank 2014, 67). The lack of an established registry can make it difficult for insolvency representatives to identify assets for recovery.

Impediments to Enforcement

In asset recovery cases, insolvency representatives may need to conduct enforcement actions to recover assets from a company's debtors. These actions may be filed directly with the bankruptcy court or in other civil or commercial courts of the jurisdiction.

Effective debt enforcement requires that the legal, tax, and regulatory elements of the framework are mutually reinforcing and work together for a timely, efficient, and cost-effective resolution. Moreover, effective debt enforcement depends on a strong institutional infrastructure, with an independent and competent judiciary that applies the law in a transparent, predictable, and consistent manner.

Other institutional elements also play a significant role. In jurisdictions where bailiffs oversee enforcement, they must be adequately trained, supervised, and paid. If bailiffs are paid in advance, adequate incentives must ensure that they perform their function.

Transparency and Accountability of Legal Insolvency Frameworks

The bedrock of any legal process is transparency of decision making and accountability of all participants. Many developing countries do not publish lower court decisions, and in some jurisdictions, appellate court decisions are published only selectively or sporadically; both have consequences for the recovery of assets through the insolvency process. First, parties will have little recourse in the event of a questionable decision by a judge. Second, the inability to consult precedent makes it difficult for litigants to predict how a court might rule and deprives judges of the means of developing consistent rulings on similar issues.

The level of accountability in the court system can be an issue in developing countries. Inefficiencies and delays can result when judges are not accountable to a chief justice who can monitor progress on cases and set time standards. A lack of accountability also affects the functioning of judicial officers, such as registrars and bailiffs, who may play an important role in litigation in many developing jurisdictions.

Recognition and Use of Laws and Proceedings in Cross-Border Insolvency

Many large corporations and individuals have international operations or customers and suppliers throughout the world. Corruption and asset recovery cases often involve assets, individuals, or entities located in a jurisdiction different from the jurisdiction in which the insolvency litigation was begun. This section provides an overview of the legal tools that enable the use or enforcement of insolvency legislation and orders in cross-border cases.

The UNCITRAL Model Law on Cross-Border Insolvency

Many countries have adopted or enacted legislation to ensure transnational consistency in the application and enforcement of cross-border insolvency laws. In 1997, the United Nations Commission on International Trade Law (UNCITRAL) adopted the Model

Law on Cross-Border Insolvency (Model Law), to provide "effective mechanisms for dealing with cases of cross-border insolvency" (UNCITRAL 2014, 3). The Model Law promotes, among other things, "cooperation between the courts and other competent authorities of [the adopting] State and foreign States involved in cases of cross-border insolvency" (UNCITRAL 2014, 3). In 2013, UNCITRAL added the Guide to Enactment and Interpretation, which provides commentary on the provisions of the Model Law (UNCITRAL 2014).

As of 2019, the Model Law has been adopted in 44 states in 46 jurisdictions, including Australia, the British Virgin Islands, Canada, Colombia, Gibraltar, Japan, Kenya, Mexico, New Zealand, the Republic of Korea, Singapore, South Africa, the United Kingdom, the U.S. Virgin Islands, and the United States.[3] Many of the signatories have adopted individual variations that are beyond the scope of this chapter.

The Model Law includes provisions that are intended to facilitate the orderly administration of cross-border insolvency estates. The first is access—giving foreign representatives and creditors of the insolvent person or entity access to the courts of the enacting jurisdiction to seek relief in the local and other jurisdictions. The second is recognition—a speedy and cost-effective method of qualifying and legitimizing both the foreign proceeding and the representative of that proceeding. To facilitate recognition, the Model Law introduces the "center of main interest" (COMI), from which the debtor conducts the administration of its business on a regular basis. The third is specifically delineated relief, both on an interim basis and upon recognition, to identify the applicable law and governing jurisdiction and reduce the risk and cost of litigating the impact of foreign law on the recognition procedure. The fourth is cooperation—to empower local and foreign courts to communicate and jointly address issues raised in the administration of cross-border insolvencies. (In July 2018, the UNCITRAL adopted a Model Law on Recognition and Enforcement of Insolvency-Related Judgments.)

The Model Law has not yet been adopted by many European nations. Regulation (EU) 2015/848 of the European Parliament and of the Council of May 20, 2015, on Insolvency Proceedings (EU Regulation), provides a framework of common rules on cross-border insolvency proceedings applicable to European Union (EU) Member States.

The Model Law was, however, codified in the United States as chapter 15 of the U.S. Bankruptcy Code, enacted in 2005.[4] Under chapter 15, recognition requires the filing of a petition by a judicial administrator, insolvency representative, or similar representative appointed by a foreign court or body.[5] A certified copy of the order commencing the proceedings and appointing the foreign representative must be included with the filing. (Other more detailed procedural steps are beyond the scope of this chapter.) The petition must allege a foreign judicial proceeding for the restructuring or liquidation of debts and assets in a foreign court and that the affairs of the debtor are subject to the supervision of a foreign court. The petition must also allege that the foreign proceeding is a foreign main or nonmain proceeding and that the foreign representative applying for recognition is a person, defined as including both individuals and juridical entities.[6] If the requirements are met, there is a strong presumption that the foreign proceeding will be granted recognition. Courts may, nevertheless, deny recognition that would be "manifestly contrary to the public policy of the United States."[7]

The remainder of this section describes the Model Law as adopted in the United Kingdom and the United States, which use similar legal and procedural methods for obtaining cross-border recognition and maintaining open communication between courts.

Foreign Main Recognition

A debtor's COMI determines whether a foreign proceeding will be granted "foreign main" or "foreign nonmain" recognition, which are accompanied by greater or lesser rights, respectively. Foreign main recognition is granted to a "collective judicial proceeding under a law relating to insolvency or adjustment of debts" that is "pending in the country where the debtor has the center of [its] main interests or establishment."[8] Section 1516 of the U.S. Bankruptcy Code further provides that, in the absence of evidence to the contrary, the bankruptcy court may presume that the bankrupt debtor's COMI is the location of its registered office, if an entity, or the habitual residence of a person.[9] The Bankruptcy Code does not define "habitual residence" but the term is understood to imply "an element of permanence and stability and is comparable to domicile; it connotes a meaningful connection to a jurisdiction, a home base where an individual lives, raises a family, works, and has ties to the community."[10] "Habitual residence" has also been defined as the place where a person resides with the intent to remain indefinitely. In determining a debtor's COMI, courts have considered factors such as the debtor's immigration status, "the location of a debtor's primary assets; the location of the majority of the debtor's creditors or [where] a majority of creditors would be affected by the case; and the jurisdiction whose law would apply to most disputes."[11]

Foreign Nonmain Recognition

A foreign nonmain proceeding is one that is pending in a jurisdiction where the debtor has an establishment, but which is not its COMI.[12] An establishment is "any place of operations where the debtor carries out a nontransitory economic activity."[13] A "place of operations" is a place from which the debtor conducts economic activities, whether the activities are commercial, industrial, or professional.[14] To determine the establishment of an individual debtor, courts have looked to the legislative history of the European Union Convention on Insolvency Proceedings on which the drafters of the Model Law relied: if a claim of primary place of business abroad is rejected, a secondary place of business or a secondary residence constitutes an establishment.

Public Policy Exception to Recognition

A bankruptcy court may refuse to recognize a foreign proceeding if it believes doing so would be "manifestly contrary to public policy of the United States."[15] This provision, included in the Model Law, enables bankruptcy courts not to follow chapter 15 if doing so would contradict fundamental principles of U.S. law, particularly statutory and constitutional guarantees.[16]

By its use of the term "manifestly," the U.S. Congress intended that this provision be interpreted restrictively and "invoked only under exceptional circumstances concerning matters of fundamental importance to the United States."[17] Courts should consider "(1) whether the foreign proceeding was procedurally unfair; and (2) whether the application of foreign law or the recognition of foreign main proceeding under Chapter 15 would 'severely impinge the value and import' of a U.S. statutory or constitutional right such that granting comity would 'severely hinder United States bankruptcy courts' abilities to carry out . . . the most fundamental policies and purposes of these rights."[18] Another court concluded: "Significantly, the fact that application of foreign law leads to a different result than application of U.S. law is, without more, insufficient to support §1506 protection, . . . [as] the whole purpose of Chapter 15 would be defeated if local or parochial interests routinely trumped the foreign law of the main proceeding."[19] The cases in which U.S. courts have found that recognition is unavailable on the basis of public policy concerns had facts in which affirmative violations of law had been committed or were being asked for.[20]

Relief Under Chapter 15 Upon Recognition

The recognition of a foreign main proceeding confers on the foreign representative immediate remedies and powers,[21] including the automatic stay provided for under the Bankruptcy Code of all proceedings against the debtor or the property of the debtor and the ability of the foreign representative to operate the debtor's business. The automatic stay prohibits creditors from pursuing actions against the debtor or its assets to satisfy debts owed to them, and, absent exigent circumstances, the stay remains in effect until the close of the foreign main proceeding.[22] The automatic stay has four main purposes: (1) to stop collection efforts, which gives the debtor time to devise a plan to resolve the financial situation that caused the insolvency; (2) to permit the foreign representative to collect the debtor's assets and liquidate them for the benefit of all creditors; (3) to give assurance to all creditors that other creditors are not pursuing independent remedies (either judicial or nonjudicial) to drain the debtor's assets; and (4) to harmonize the interests of the creditors and the debtor.

Upon a main or nonmain recognition, the court, at its discretion, may also (1) grant a stay of proceedings and execution of judgment against the debtor that might otherwise fall outside the scope of the automatic stay; (2) provide for the right to request documentation and oral testimony "concerning the debtor's assets, affairs, rights, obligations or liabilities"; and (3) authorize the foreign representative to administer the asset of the debtor within the United States.[23] The ability to obtain discovery in a chapter 15 proceeding[24] is national in scope and so broad it has been described by several courts as a court-sanctioned fishing expedition.[25]

Remedies not Available Under the U.S. Bankruptcy Code

The U.S. Bankruptcy Code and the insolvency laws of most countries provide for "avoidance actions," pursuant to which preferential transfers, transfers for insufficient value, and certain other unauthorized transfers may be cancelled and the transferred assets or their value recovered for the benefit of creditors.[26] Upon the avoidance of a transfer, either the property transferred or its value must be returned to the bankruptcy estate.[27] In a chapter 15 proceeding, a foreign representative may initiate an avoidance action only if it is based on state or foreign law (as opposed to federal bankruptcy law).[28]

Section 1509 (comparable to the right of direct access under article 9 of the Model Law) places restrictions on a foreign representative's access to local courts. Although section 1509(a) permits a foreign representative to file a petition for recognition "directly with the court," section 1509(d) states that, if recognition is denied under chapter 15, the court may issue "any appropriate order necessary to prevent the foreign representative from obtaining comity or cooperation from courts in the United States." Section 1509(f) further states that, although a foreign representative *need not* proceed under chapter 15 to have standing to sue in the United States, a denial of recognition under chapter 15 carries the risk that later attempts to seek comity and cooperation from U.S. courts will be barred.

United Kingdom Cross-Border Insolvency Regulations 2006

The United Kingdom adopted the Model Law in 2006 as the Cross-Border Insolvency Regulations 2006 (2006 Regulations). The 2006 Regulations are intended to supplement rather than replace the EU Regulation, to which, as of mid-2019, the United Kingdom remained subject. In the event of a conflict between the 2006 Regulations and the EU Regulation, the EU Regulation controls. The effect of Brexit on this issue has not been settled.

In large part, the 2006 Regulations adhere to the language and concepts of the Model Law. There are, however, several key distinctions:

- First, the 2006 Regulations vary from the Model Law to account for the British court system, the different forms of relief available under British insolvency law, and to clarify the provisions of the automatic stay following recognition.
- Second, the 2006 Regulations deny relief to numerous companies regulated or protected by separate legislation, such as certain public companies, insurance providers, U.K. credit institutions, and protected railway companies.
- Third, where permissible domestically under the U.K. Insolvency Act 1986, notification to foreign creditors of the ancillary proceeding may be made by advertisement in foreign newspapers chosen by the foreign representative.

Finally, unlike their U.S. counterpart, the 2006 Regulations do not preempt or exclude a foreign representative from applying for relief under the predecessor section 426 of the U.K. Insolvency Act 1986, *Co-operations Between Courts Exercising Jurisdiction in Relation to Insolvency*, or under the common law. Section 426 applies to insolvency proceedings in the courts of Australia, the Bahamas, the British Virgin Islands, the Cayman Islands, the Channel Islands, Ireland, the Isle of Man, and

New Zealand, among others. Petitions for recognition and relief are often made in the alternative under the various statutory provisions in cross-border insolvencies.

International and Institutional Considerations

International Considerations

To enable the recovery of assets, a country's legal system should embody the recognized best practices of World Bank Principle C15 (box 5.1). A predictable and robust cross-border system is critical for the tracking and retrieval of stolen assets because these cases often involve multiple jurisdictions.

Cross-border insolvency agreements should be permitted and encouraged. World Bank Principle C17.5 on Cross-Border Insolvency Agreements provides: "The system should permit insolvency representatives and other parties in interest to enter into cross-border insolvency agreements involving two or more enterprise group members in different States, in order to facilitate coordination of the proceedings. The system should allow the courts to approve or implement such agreements."

Institutional Considerations

Institutional capacity varies widely across jurisdictions. A country's legislative framework may be less important than the status of the judiciary and the rule of law (box 5.2).

The World Bank has issued principles for the development of adequate institutional frameworks (box 5.3).

BOX 5.1   **World Bank Principle C15: International Considerations**

Insolvency proceedings may have international aspects, and a country's legal system should establish clear rules pertaining to jurisdiction, recognition of foreign judgments, cooperation among courts in different countries, and choice of law. Key factors relating to effective handling of cross-border matters typically include:

- A clear and speedy process for obtaining recognition of foreign insolvency proceedings;

- Relief to be granted upon recognition of foreign insolvency proceedings;

- Foreign insolvency representatives to have access to courts and other relevant authorities;

- Courts and insolvency representatives to cooperate in international insolvency proceedings; and

- Nondiscrimination between foreign and domestic creditors.

World Bank Principle D1: Implementation—Institutional and Regulatory Frameworks

D1.1: Independence, Impartiality, and Effectiveness. The system should guarantee the independence of the judiciary. Judicial decisions should be impartial. Courts should act in a competent manner and effectively.

D1.2: Role of Courts in Insolvency Proceedings. Insolvency proceedings should be overseen and impartially disposed of by an independent court and assigned, where practical, to judges with specialized insolvency expertise. Nonjudicial institutions playing judicial roles in insolvency proceedings should be subject to the same principles and standards applied to the judiciary.

D3: Court Organization. The court should be organized so that all interested parties—including the attorneys, the insolvency representative, the debtor, the creditors, the public, and the media—are dealt with fairly, in a timely manner, objectively, and as part of an efficient, transparent system. Implicit in that structure are firm and recognized lines of authority, clear allocation of tasks and responsibilities, and orderly operations in the court.

World Bank Principles and Best Practices

In 2001, the World Bank and UNCITRAL, in consultation with the International Monetary Fund, designed the Insolvency and Creditor Rights Standard (the ICR Standard) to represent the international consensus on best practices for evaluating and strengthening national insolvency and creditor rights systems. The ICR Standard combines the World Bank Principles for Effective Insolvency and Creditor/Debtor Regimes (the World Bank Principles) and the UNCITRAL Legislative Guide on Insolvency Law (UNCITRAL 2004). The Financial Stability Board, which monitors and assesses vulnerabilities in the global financial system, has recognized the ICR Standard and designated the UNCITRAL and the World Bank as joint standard setters in the area of insolvency.

The World Bank Principles emphasize contextual, integrated solutions and the policy choices available for the development of those solutions. The World Bank Principles constitute the international best practices in the design of insolvency systems and creditor-debtor regimes. Adapting international best practices to the realities of individual jurisdictions requires an understanding of the market environments in which these systems operate, especially in developing jurisdictions, where common challenges include weak or unclear social protection mechanisms, weak financial institutions and capital markets, ineffective corporate governance and uncompetitive businesses, ineffective or weak laws, institutions and regulation, and a shortage of capacity and resources. These obstacles pose challenges to the adoption of systems that address the needs of developing countries while keeping pace with global trends and good practices. The application of the World Bank Principles in a jurisdiction will be influenced by domestic policy choices.

(continued next page)

BOX 5.3   World Bank Principles and Best Practices *(continued)*

The effective functioning of the insolvency framework depends on both the substantive legal and regulatory systems and institutional factors. Institutions are the vital foundation on which the insolvency framework is based. Without effective institutions—judicial and administrative—the insolvency system can be unpredictable, slow, and unfair. The institutional framework has three main elements: (1) the institutions responsible for insolvency proceedings; (2) the operational system through which cases and decisions are processed; and (3) the requirements needed to preserve the integrity of those institutions, because the integrity of the insolvency system is the linchpin of its success. Several fundamental principles influence the design and maintenance of the institutions and participants with authority over insolvency proceedings.

The Conflict between State Confiscation of Criminal Assets and Insolvency Proceedings

Cross-border insolvency processes raise many complex issues. The pursuit of assets in a variety of jurisdictions requires careful strategic planning, especially when the laws of the different jurisdictions diverge. As a general rule, the location of assets will determine the applicable law. In some jurisdictions, assets held locally may be ring-fenced under local insolvency law giving creditors within that jurisdiction first priority.

In international corruption cases, assets may be the subject of a preservation order under the criminal law of a jurisdiction or under a mutual legal assistance treaty (MLAT) request from a foreign country. In such cases, assets may be held or "preserved" for years pending the conclusion of all criminal appeals abroad, removing the potential assets of an insolvent estate from the insolvency representative's balance sheet. Insolvency practitioners and law enforcement should attempt to cooperate to benefit both creditors and the victims of crime.

The conflict between criminal and bankruptcy proceedings was reflected in the wave of bankruptcies following the collapse of a series of Ponzi schemes in the United States in 2008 (Bernard Madoff—$18 billion; Tom Petters—$3.6 billion); 2009 (Robert Alan Stanford—$5.5 billion; Nevin Shapiro—$880 million; Scott Rothstein—$1 billion); and 2012 (Nikolai Battoo—$500 million). In these cases, conflicts arose between the U.S. federal criminal or civil asset forfeiture laws and the distributive regime of the U.S. Bankruptcy Code. For example, victims of fraud may be entitled to file a petition for remission of monies forfeited to the United States as the proceeds of crime entirely outside traditional bankruptcy proceedings. These petitions may be in direct conflict with the policies of rateable distribution and "absolute priority" under the U.S. Bankruptcy Code. Also, a "victim" in a criminal case may be a "creditor" under bankruptcy law; but not all creditors are victims under criminal asset forfeiture law (compare, for example, a trade creditor with an investor in a Ponzi scheme).

A criminal asset forfeiture order can have the effect of removing assets from the pool of value available to an insolvency estate that would otherwise be available for rateable distribution to creditors. Likewise, assets held by third parties that would otherwise be subject to claw-back provisions under bankruptcy law may also be unavailable. In some cases, a debtor who is also a criminal defendant in pending proceedings may voluntarily turn over assets in settlement of a restitution action, fine, or penalty that are then used to compensate victims in preference to creditors who would have had rights under a bankruptcy distribution scheme.

When a debtor faces criminal charges, state forfeiture provisions can interfere with assets that would otherwise be subject to the jurisdiction of the court in which the insolvency or bankruptcy proceedings are being administered. State forfeiture provisions can also interfere with distributions from the bankruptcy estate. In many jurisdictions, upon commencement of an insolvency or bankruptcy case, all civil actions against the debtor are automatically stayed. The stay does not necessarily apply, however, to asset forfeiture proceedings commenced by the state. In the United States, for example, because forfeiture is considered punishment for a crime, forfeiture proceedings are not automatically stayed by a U.S. Bankruptcy Court filing by or against a debtor. The tension between insolvency proceedings and criminal asset forfeiture is illustrated by *Stanford International Bank* in box 5.4.

In the United States, title to assets obtained through a criminal offense that are forfeited to the state are removed from the reach of bankruptcy because ownership of such assets is considered to have been transferred as of the date of the crime. A bankrupt estate consists of the assets of the debtor as of the date of commencement of bankruptcy (subject to the power to avoid fraudulent dispositions); assets forfeited as a result of a crime that occurred prior to the commencement of bankruptcy are not included. An order forfeiting funds in a bank account does not, however, forfeit funds that the debtor had previously paid from that account to third parties. A trustee in bankruptcy may assert claw-back claims and recover those funds. A criminal or civil asset forfeiture order does not divest a bankruptcy trustee of such claims. A claimant who can establish sufficient evidence of his legal interest in the property or who can establish that the property is subject to a constructive trust[29] may be able to supersede a forfeiture order.

BOX 5.4   The Stanford International Bank (in Liquidation)

Stanford International Bank (SIB), based in the Caribbean, went into receivership in 2009 when its parent company, the Stanford Financial Group was seized by U.S. authorities as part of the investigation into Allen Stanford (see the section titled *Claims against Corporate Officers, Agents, and Third-Party Facilitators* in chapter 3).

Under U.K. law, when a conflict arises between creditors' rights and the state's interest in confiscation of the proceeds of crime, victim creditors may be

(continued next page)

BOX 5.4   The Stanford International Bank (in Liquidation) *(continued)*

prejudiced if the state obtains a restraining order. A restraining order will prohibit the debtor from transferring assets to its victim creditors unless the creditors (or the insolvency representative) can establish a proprietary claim to the property stolen and bring themselves within the definition of a "third party" who "holds property" frozen by a restraining order. The restraining order will remain in force even if a debtor is prepared to repay all or part of the stolen funds. A preliminary decision of the English Court of Appeal of 2010 in *Re Stanford International Bank*[a] provisionally resolved the issue of whether $100 million in frozen sums should remain frozen or be released to foreign insolvency representatives acting on behalf of 22,000 creditor victims. The court held that the funds should remain frozen. The state was in a position to conduct an orderly distribution at the conclusion of the criminal proceedings, and a contrary policy could lead to a scramble by victims and insolvency representatives to secure the distribution of funds to satisfy their claims to the debtor's assets in preference to others.

In July 2011, however, Mrs. Justice Elizabeth Gloster of the English High Court released $20 million of the $100 million in frozen funds to the Antiguan insolvency representatives of SIB. These were considered "living expenses" needed to allow the Antiguan estate to preserve and pursue $5.5 billion in ancillary civil liability damages claims against certain banks, law firms, and other facilitators of the Stanford fraud before the statutes of limitation on such claims expired and to fund other asset recovery work. Mrs. Justice Gloster also indicated that the Antiguan insolvency representatives' claim to have been vested with the title to the remaining $80 million in frozen assets in London (by means of their appointment as insolvency representatives in April 2009 and by reason of the operation of Antiguan law vesting title to SIB's assets in the names of its insolvency representatives) prior to the July 30, 2009, issuance of an external Proceeds of Crime Act restraint order (upon an MLAT request from the U.S. Department of Justice (DOJ)), was likely to prevail.

In March 2013, the DOJ, the U.S. Securities and Exchange Commission (SEC), an SEC receiver, and the Antiguan insolvency representatives of SIB entered into a Settlement Agreement and Cross-Border Cooperation Protocol, which resolved the conflict between state-driven criminal asset forfeiture proceedings and the cross-border insolvency process. The DOJ, acting with the U.K.'s Serious Fraud Office, the Office of Justice in Bern, Switzerland, and the Attorney General of Ontario, sought to recover more than $300 million of bank deposits frozen in Canada, the United Kingdom, and Switzerland. The Antiguan insolvency representatives sought to use a portion of the available frozen funds to develop and pursue $5.5 billion in predominantly ancillary civil liability actions against banks, law firms, and other enablers of the fraud, including against Toronto-Dominion Bank for negligence and knowing assistance. Evidence has since been shared and cooperation is ongoing between the SEC receiver and the Antiguan insolvency representatives of SIB. The compromise between the parties may result in a substantially greater recovery.

a. [2010] EWCA Civ. 137.

A constructive trust is an equitable remedy imposed by a court to benefit a party that has been wrongfully deprived of its rights by another's obtaining or holding a legal property right through unjust enrichment or interference or through a breach of fiduciary duty. If the imposition of a trust is likely to affect the recovery of other victims from a limited pool of forfeiture assets, however, U.S. courts may conclude that the remedy is inequitable and refuse to allow the claimant to recover.[30]

In cases of corruption, the state may be the beneficial owner of public funds or assets that were misappropriated, including any profits derived from that property or any property into which it has been converted. Beneficial ownership adheres unless there is a bona fide purchaser for value without notice of the breach of trust. Saadi Qaddafi used funds belonging to Libya to purchase a $10 million property in London. The property was owned by a shell company of which Qaddafi was the beneficial owner. The English High Court found that Qaddafi held the house in constructive trust and ordered its transfer to Libya.[31]

Article 53 of the United Nations Convention Against Corruption (UNCAC) requires states to permit the initiation of civil actions by other state parties to establish ownership of property acquired through corruption and to recognize another state's claim as the beneficial owner. A successful state claimant in a property-based action will have priority over the defendant's other creditors (van der Does de Willebois and Brun 2013).

Criminal and civil asset forfeiture procedures have weaknesses; some jurisdictions lack a provision entitling general unsecured creditors, such as trade creditors, to be compensated from forfeited funds. Trustees and receivers can, however, seek to avoid certain asset transfers and may also seek recovery for damages. The benefits of having all assets (whether tangible or intangible, including the rights to sue facilitators of fraud or corruption) marshalled under the insolvency representative or the receiver have been recognized by courts, such as the Seventh Circuit Court of Appeals in *United States v. Frykholm*,[32] in which Judge Easterbrook commented:

> Neither side paid much attention to the effect of the fraudulent conveyance, likely because both sides are represented by forfeiture specialists and have focused on the language of § 853 and opinions interpreting that statute. Everything would have been clearer had the United States initiated an involuntary bankruptcy proceeding against Frykholm. That not only would have brought to the fore § 548 of the Bankruptcy Code but also would have provided a superior way to marshal Frykholm's remaining assets and distribute them to her creditors. Although § 853(n)(1) allows the Attorney General to use forfeited assets for restitution, it does not create a comprehensive means of collecting and distributing assets. Bankruptcy would have made it pellucid that Cotswold cannot enjoy any priority over the other victims and cannot reap a profit while Frykholm's other creditors go begging. Moreover, bankruptcy would have enabled the trustee to recoup the sums distributed to the first generation of investors, who received $5 million or so against $2.5 million paid in. Those payments could have been reclaimed under the trustee's avoiding powers and made available to all of the bilked investors.[33]

In *SEC v. Madoff*,[34] Judge Stanton, in commenting on the opposition to an application to modify a preliminary injunction to allow a group of creditors to file an involuntary bankruptcy petition against Mr. Madoff, stated:

> No opponent to the relief sought by the motion offers as familiar, comprehensive, and experienced a regime as does the Bankruptcy Code for staying the proliferation of individual lawsuits against Mr. Madoff individually, marshaling his personal assets other than those criminally forfeitable, and distributing those assets among his creditors according to an established hierarchy of claims.
>
> A Bankruptcy Trustee has direct rights to Mr. Madoff's individual property, with the ability to maximize the size of the estate available to Mr. Madoff's creditors through his statutory authority to locate assets, avoid fraudulent transfers, and preserve or increase the value of assets through investment or sale, as well as provide notice to creditors, process claims, and make distributions in a transparent manner under the procedures and preferences established by Congress, all under the supervision of the Bankruptcy Court.[35]

Despite these rulings, conflicting interests continue to be an issue in forfeited property cases. Cooperation and coordination agreements between a trustee or receiver and a government have successfully mitigated some of the problems.[36] In *United States v. Petters*,[37] the court on its own motion chose to use the bankruptcy process over state-managed restitution proceedings to redress the claims of victims, noting that "it would be a waste of resources to order restitution of pennies on the dollar (at best) when most victims have filed, or will be filing, parallel claims in bankruptcy proceedings."[38] The benefits of cooperation and coordination can extend beyond the sharing of information and the decision on what can be claimed and by whom to the preservation and maximization of value for the benefit of all creditors.

Cooperation was beneficial in the chapter 11 bankruptcy of California agribusiness giant SK Foods LP, a case involving a number of jurisdictional elements (see box 5.5).

A cooperation agreement also helped resolve disputes in the bankruptcy of Banco Santos (see box 5.6).

BOX 5.5   SK Foods LP

SK Foods LP (SK Foods) was the second-largest processor of tomatoes for commercial use in the United States, with revenues of $270 million per year. Its customers included Heinz and Kraft. The business went into bankruptcy in the United States after the U.S. Federal Bureau of Investigation found evidence of price fixing, bribery, and sales of tainted tomato products. Scott Salyer, SK Foods' owner, was convicted of price-fixing and racketeering and sentenced to six years in federal prison.

SK Foods had owned several operating subsidiaries in Australia, collectively known as Cedenco. Bradley Sharp, the U.S. bankruptcy trustee, was advised by

(continued next page)

BOX 5.5   SK Foods LP *(continued)*

SK Foods' former management that SK Foods had transferred its interests in Cedenco to affiliates owned and controlled by Salyer. Audited financial statements corroborated this account. Cedenco was placed into Australian receivership shortly after the U.S. bankruptcy proceeding commenced. The Australian receivers sold its assets, paying all secured and unsecured debt in full and leaving a surplus of more than $50 million for Cedenco's owner.

Sharp determined, however, that the ownership of Cedenco had never been transferred and, therefore, Cedenco remained an asset of SK Foods. Sharp asserted ownership of Cedenco and the $50 million surplus. Salyer contested Sharp's claim and alleged that, as a result of subsequent transfers, Cedenco was owned and controlled by offshore asset-protection structures in the West Indies and the Cook Islands.

Sharp sought a determination of the ownership of Cedenco from the U.S. bankruptcy court and obtained an injunction against a series of defendants claiming an interest in Cedenco, including the offshore vehicles, thus preventing any further attempts to transfer interests in Cedenco outside the jurisdiction of the bankruptcy court. The Australian insolvency representatives refused to be bound by the U.S. injunction, risking the possibility that they would distribute assets to a Salyer entity, which would then transfer those assets to yet another entity beyond the jurisdiction of the Australian and U.S. courts.

In March 2012, Sharp obtained an order from the U.S. bankruptcy court appointing a receiver for the Salyer entities to hold any distribution received from the Australian insolvency representatives. He then sought and obtained an order from the Federal Court of Australia recognizing the U.S. bankruptcy court's receivership order. In August 2012, Sharp succeeded in obtaining a summary judgment from the U.S. bankruptcy court that he, as trustee, owned Cedenco under Australian law because there had been no transfer of title to the shares of Cedenco prior to bankruptcy.

Because the Salyer entities and Australian insolvency representatives refused to acknowledge the judgment of the U.S. bankruptcy court as to his ownership, as trustee, of Cedenco, Sharp sought a judgment from the Federal Court of Australia recognizing his ownership rights. In 2013, the Australian Court found that the Salyer entities were estopped from relitigating the issues that had been decided by the U.S. bankruptcy court and recognized Sharp as the owner in trust of Cedenco.

It might have appeared that the Australian judgment cleared the way for the repatriation of the Cedenco proceeds. Prior to the court's decision, however, the Australian Federal Police made an application under the Australian Proceeds of Crime Act to prohibit the payment to Sharp, and declare the funds forfeit, claiming that they represented the proceeds of Salyer's criminal activity in the United States.

Had the criminal asset forfeiture action been successful, the creditors would have suffered because the Australian government would not have been required to use the proceeds to compensate victims of Salyer's crimes. The Australian

(continued next page)

BOX 5.5   SK Foods LP *(continued)*

Federal Police admitted that any forfeited funds would be used for other purposes. Sharp engaged in a concerted campaign to convince all parties that forfeiture would result in an injustice to the real victims, the creditors. He mobilized various U.S. senators and members of the California congressional delegation and conducted a forensic accounting analysis that showed the link between the funds and Salyer's criminal activities in the United States.

Before the initial forfeiture hearing, Sharp and the Australian Federal Police agreed to mediation and reached a settlement. Sharp convinced not only the Australian Federal Police, but also the DOJ, the U.S. Department of State, and legislators in California that the creditors would be hurt by the criminal asset forfeiture effort. The Australian Federal Police agreed to release 90 percent of the Cedenco proceeds, with the remainder to be deposited into the Commonwealth of Australia's Confiscated Assets Account. The Australian Federal Police also agreed to support Sharp's application to release the remaining proceeds for the benefit of SK Foods' creditors.

BOX 5.6   Banco Santos

Banco Santos, a Brazilian bank, became insolvent as a result of acts of fraud by its main shareholder, Edemar Cid Ferreira. Dr. Eronides Aparecido Rodrigues dos Santos, the Public Attorney, petitioned the bankruptcy court in Brazil for an order to pierce the corporate veil of Banco Santos and to extend the bankruptcy to several other entities, ultimately owned by Ferreira, that benefited from the diversion of assets from Banco Santos. Prosecutors had also filed a criminal complaint against Ferreira and obtained a seizure order against all the assets controlled by his entities, including those entities subject to the order piercing the corporate veil.

Those entities, now part of the bankruptcy estate, owned works of art in the United States that had previously been frozen pursuant to an MLAT issued by the Brazilian prosecutors. A conflict arose between the insolvency estate and the Brazilian criminal court. The insolvency estate sought to recover the art to compensate the victims of the bankruptcy, and the criminal court sought to confiscate the same assets for a state museum. Minister Massami Uyeada of the Superior Court of Brazil, the highest court for federal matters, ruled that the assets owned by the entities behind the corporate veil, although frozen by the criminal court, be transferred to the insolvency estate and used to compensate the victims of the bankruptcy. The court affirmed that frozen assets do not remain with the state, even if the seizure order was issued before the insolvency began.

After the judicial dispute in Brazil was resolved, the bankruptcy court and the criminal court had to collaborate to repatriate the assets to Brazil. Only the criminal court had the authority to carry out the MLAT. The bankruptcy court and the criminal court entered into a Term of Adjustment of Competencies and Mutual Cooperation. Under that agreement, the criminal court would fulfill the MLAT and, upon receiving the assets, transfer them to the insolvency estate.

Key Points from this Chapter

- In many developing countries, outdated insolvency laws remain on the books, and there is limited or no local experience in conducting insolvency cases. These jurisdictions may face challenges in implementing insolvency as a tool to support cross-border asset recovery.

- Many countries have enacted legislation to ensure transnational consistency and proper oversight in the application and enforcement of cross-border insolvency laws.

- A country's legal system should ideally have clear rules pertaining to jurisdiction, recognition of foreign judgments, cooperation among courts in different countries, and choice of law.

- The pursuit of assets in a variety of jurisdictions requires careful strategic planning, especially where applicable laws diverge.

Notes

1. Although there can be overlap between offshore jurisdictions and developing countries, as used in this chapter offshore jurisdictions are those that provide financial services to nonresidents that are out of proportion to the size of their domestic economy, whether or not they would also be considered developing countries.
2. Using another indicator of court efficiency, resolving a contractual dispute takes, on average, 1,109 days in South Asia and 768.5 days in Latin America and the Caribbean (World Bank 2018).
3. UNCITRAL (United Nations Commission on International Trade Law), Status of Model Law on Cross-Border Insolvency with Guide to Enactment, UNCITRAL, Vienna (accessed August 5, 2019), http://www.uncitral.org/uncitral/en/uncitral_texts/insolvency/1997Model_status.html; Regulation (EU) 2015/848 of the European Parliament and of the Council of May 20, 2015, on Insolvency Proceedings, annex A, https://eur-lex.europa.eu/legal-content/EN/TXT/HTML/?uri=CELEX:32015R0848&from=en.
4. 11 U.S.C. §§ 1501–1532 (2019). These provisions repealed and replaced 11 U.S.C. § 304, *Cases Ancillary to Foreign Proceedings*, which had been in effect since 1978.
5. Federal Rule of Bankruptcy Procedure 1007.
6. 11 U.S.C. § 1517; 11 U.S.C. § 101.
7. Ibid. § 1506.
8. Ibid. §§ 1502(4), 1515–1517.
9. Ibid. § 1516(c).
10. In re Kemsley, 489 B.R. 346, 353 (Bankr. S.D.N.Y. 2013).
11. See, for example, In re Loy, 380 B.R. 154, 162 (Bankr. E.D. Va. 2007) (recognizing the United Kingdom as the COMI where a debtor had only temporary legal status in the United States, almost all the debtor's creditors were located in the United Kingdom, and English law governed the debtor's initial proposal for voluntary

reorganization with his U.K. creditors, as well as a later bankruptcy proceeding); In re Chiang, 437 B.R. 397, 404 (Bankr. C.D. Cal. 2010) (recognizing a Canadian bankruptcy case as a foreign main proceeding because the debtor's permanent legal status in Canada and his strong personal ties indicated that Canada was his COMI).

12. 11 U.S.C. §§ 1502(5), 1515–1517.

13. Ibid. § 1502 (2).

14. In re Ran, 607 F.3d 1017 (5th Cir. 2010).

15. 11 U.S.C. § 1506.

16. H.R. Rep. No. 109-31 (2005).

17. In re British American Isle of Venice (BVI), Ltd., 441 B.R. 713, 717 (Bankr. S.D. Fla. 2010) (rejecting a public policy challenge to recognition based on allegations of purported procedural unfairness of foreign proceedings due to a claimed conflict of interest and confidentiality order with another creditor when the complaining party was afforded the right to appear and defend in the foreign proceedings, and, although a conflict of interest may lead to disqualification under U.S. law, it did not under British Virgin Islands law).

18. Ibid. See also In re Fairfield Sentry Ltd., 714 F.3d 127 (2d Cir. 2013) (public policy exception cannot be invoked based on the argument that the British Virgin Islands proceedings were cloaked in secrecy and under seal because confidentiality does not offend U.S. public policy, the complaining party had the right in the British Virgin Islands to seek leave to access sealed documents, and "unfettered public access to court records is [not] so fundamental in the United States" as to justify denial of recognition); In re Millard, 501 B.R. 644 (Bankr. S.D.N.Y. 2013) (rejecting a § 1506 challenge based on a stay of judgment and potential rejection of default judgment for unpaid taxes by the Cayman Islands court when, among other things, similar laws applied under U.S. law and bad faith in allegedly seeking to avoid judgment, even if it could be found, rejecting as not ripe for consideration a § 1506 challenge based on a stay of judgment and potential rejection of default judgment for unpaid taxes by the Cayman Islands court, even if bad faith in allegedly seeking to avoid judgment under U.S. law could be found).

19. In re Qimonda AG, 462 B.R. 165, 183-84 (Bankr. E.D. Va. 2011) (denying a motion to excuse a trustee from compliance with a section 1522 of the Bankruptcy Code prohibiting cancellation of patent-licensee contracts on public policy grounds when the provision was enacted by Congress immediately following a decision allowing avoidance of such contracts; Congress's action was based on the effect avoidance of such contracts would have on American innovation and technology, which would impinge on a *statutory* protection fundamental to U.S. public policy). See also In re Gerova Financial Group, Ltd., 482 B.R. 86, 94–95 (Bankr. S.D.N.Y. 2012) (rejecting a § 1506 public policy objection to recognition notwithstanding that under U.S. law an involuntary petition requires at least three creditors while the winding up at issue was commenced by one creditor, as permitted by Bermuda law).

20. In re Toft, 453 B.R. 186 (Bankr. S.D.N.Y. 2011) (rejecting on §1506 grounds a request for access to debtor's emails held on two Internet service provider servers and a request to place a wiretap on such email servers without giving notice to debtor as violative of the Federal Wiretap Act, the Privacy Act, and notice requirements under the rules of bankruptcy); In re Gold & Honey, Ltd., 410 B.R. 357 (Bankr. E.D.N.Y. 2009)

(denying relief to a creditor who, notwithstanding an automatic stay imposed by U.S. proceedings and a warning that proceeding abroad would be at his own risk, filed and prosecuted a proceeding in Israel as an end-run around, and in violation of, a § 362 automatic stay under the Bankruptcy Code); Jaffe v. Samsung Electronics Co., Ltd., 737 F.3d 1426, 28–29 (4th Cir. 2013) (denying a motion to excuse a trustee from compliance with a provision of Bankruptcy Code that prohibits cancellation of patent-licensee contracts on the basis of § 1522, though recognizing that by so holding it was furthering the public policy of the statutory provision that prevented cancellation of licenses) (affirming Qimonda).

21. 11 U.S.C. § 1520.
22. In re Daewoo Logistics Corp., 461 B.R. 175 (Bankr. S.D.N.Y. 2011).
23. 11 U.S.C. § 1521.
24. Federal Rule of Civil Procedure 2004.
25. See In re MMH Automotive Grp., LLC, 346 B.R. 229, 233 (Bankr. S.D. Fla. 2006) ("Rule 2004 does allow the Trustee to go on a general fishing expedition so long as the information sought relates to 'the acts, conduct, or property or to the liabilities and financial condition of the debtor, or to any matter which may affect the administration of the debtor's estate.'"); In re Washington Mutual, Inc., 408 B.R. 45, 50 (Bankr. D. Del. 2009) ("A Rule 2004 examination 'is commonly recognized as more in the nature of a 'fishing expedition.'" (citing In re Bennett Funding, Inc., 203 B.R. 24, 28 (Bankr. N.D.N.Y. 1996))); In re Marathe, 459 B.R. 850, 858–59 (Bankr. M.D. Fla. 2011) (Rule 2004 discovery "is properly extended to creditors and third parties who have had dealings with the debtor").
26. 11 U.S.C. §§ 546–550.
27. Ibid. §§ 550–551.
28. Fogerty v. Petroquest Resources, Inc. (In re Condor Ins. Ltd.), 601 F.3d 319 (5th Cir. 2010).
29. See, for example, United States v. Shefton, 548 F.3d 1360, 1366 (11th Cir. 2008); United States v. $4,224,958.57, 392 F.3d 1002, 1004–05 (9th Cir. 2004); United States v. Schwimmer, 968 F.2d 1570, 1574, 1582 (2d Cir. 1992); United States v. Marx, 844 F.2d 1303, 1308 (7th Cir. 1988); United States v. Campos, 859 F.2d 1233, 1238–39 (6th Cir. 1988).
30. See, for example, United States v. Andrews, 530 F.3d 1232, 1238–39 (10th Cir. 2008); United States v. Durham, 86 F.3d 70, 73 (5th Cir. 1996).
31. Libya v. Capitana Seas Ltd. [2012] EWHC 602 (Com).
32. 362 F.3d 413 (7th Cir. 2004).
33. Ibid. 417.
34. SEC v. Madoff, 2009 U.S. Dist. LEXIS 30712 (S.D.N.Y. Apr. 10, 2009).
35. Ibid. at 3–4.
36. Article 57(5) of UNCAC provides that state parties may "give special consideration to concluding agreements or mutually acceptable arrangements on a case-by-case basis, for the final disposal of confiscated property."
37. United States v. Petters, 2010 U.S. Dist. LEXIS 55040 (D. Minn. June 3, 2010).
38. Ibid. 14–15.

References

UNCITRAL (United Nations Commission on International Trade Law). 2004. *Legislative Guide on Insolvency Law*. Vienna: UNCITRAL.

———. 2014. *UNCITRAL Model Law on Cross-Border Insolvency with Guide to Enactment and Interpretation*. Vienna: UNCITRAL.

van der Does de Willebois, Emile, and Jean-Pierre Brun. 2013. "Using Civil Remedies in Corruption and Asset Recovery Cases." *Case Western Reserve Journal of International Law* 45 (3): 615.

World Bank. 2014. *Doing Business Report 2015: Going Beyond Efficiency*. Washington, DC: World Bank.

———. 2018. *Doing Business Report 2019: Training for Reform*. Washington, DC: World Bank.

Appendix A. Country-Specific Regulations for Insolvency Representatives

This appendix contains an edited version of a Survey of the Law of Recognition of Foreign Insolvency Office Holders that was distributed to 15 different jurisdictions.[1] The survey, which was designed to be relevant to creditors in India,[2] was given to us by the authors with the permission to publish. Responses from 11 jurisdictions have been included in appendix A; some have been condensed.

a. **Is recognition of foreign office holders permitted in your jurisdiction? What is the source and name or nature of the law governing the subject of recognition in your jurisdiction? Do you have one or more types of recognition (e.g., under [the United Nations Commission of International Trade Law] (UNCITRAL) there is foreign main and foreign nonmain recognition), and what are the principal differences between the two?**

Belgium: Article 16 of Regulation 2015/848 installed a system of automatic mutual recognition of insolvency proceedings in other Member States. There is no need for exequatur proceedings. Under the International Private Law Code, the situation is somewhat different. A foreign court decision will be automatically recognized provided the debtor has its main establishment in the country where the foreign court decision has been rendered. In territorial proceedings, there will be an automatic recognition if the court decision was rendered by a court in a country where the debtor has an establishment, other than his main establishment. In such a case, the recognition will be restricted to assets located in the territory of the country where the proceedings were initiated. In all other cases, an exequatur must be obtained for the foreign court decision to be recognized. For enforcement, an exequatur must be obtained in all cases. For example, if a foreign trustee wants to sell Belgian assets, he will have to request an exequatur.

British Virgin Islands: Recognition and assistance is available only under Part XIX of the Insolvency Act 2003 to office holders of nine designated countries or economies (Australia; Canada; Finland; Hong Kong SAR, China; Japan; Jersey; New Zealand; the United Kingdom; and the United States). The British Virgin Islands High Court has ruled that the common law approach to recognition and assistance does not survive generally in the British Virgin Islands in parallel with the statutory scheme (although it may be afforded to office holders from the nine designated countries or economies). Part XVIII of the Insolvency Act contains provisions based on the UNCITRAL Model Law on Cross-Border Insolvency for giving and seeking assistance in insolvency proceedings, but this Part has not been brought into force.

Hong Kong SAR, China: Yes, recognition of foreign office holders is permitted. This is based on Common Law, as there are no statutory provisions governing the recognition of foreign insolvencies or requiring the Hong Kong SAR, China Courts to cooperate with foreign Insolvency Practitioners.

Jersey: In Jersey, there are two routes to recognition of foreign officer holders: under Article 49, Bankruptcy (Désastre) (Jersey) Law 1990 or Jersey customary (common) law. The United Kingdom, Guernsey, the Isle of Man, Finland, and Australia are pre-scribed jurisdictions under the Bankruptcy (Désastre) (Jersey) Order 2006 for their willingness to provide reciprocal assistance to Jersey. An Article 49 application for for-eign recognition from a prescribed foreign court is usually granted automatically. Foreign office holders from nonprescribed jurisdictions can apply for recognition in Jersey under customary law as a matter of comity. Under both routes to recognition, the Jersey courts have regard to the rules of private international law and any UNCITRAL Model Law on Cross-Border Insolvency. Further, it has been suggested that the court take into account the following factors: jurisdiction; title to property for determination of the proper law in relation to that property; choice of law; and public policy. Generally, Jersey is prepared to accede to requests for foreign assistance insofar as these requests are consistent with its domestic laws and policies.

Singapore: Yes, recognition of foreign office holders is permitted. Such recognition may be based on common law and is at the discretion of the Singapore Courts. As of the date of publication, there are no statutory provisions governing the recognition of for-eign insolvencies or holders of insolvent foreign companies. One exception to this is where a foreign company registered in Singapore goes into liquidation in its place of incorporation—the foreign liquidator in such a case has the powers and functions of a Singapore liquidator, until a Singapore liquidator is appointed by the court. Singapore has, as of the date of publication, not as yet adopted the UNCITRAL Model Law [on Cross-Border Insolvency], although it is likely to do so, along with proposing a new bill which would include provisions relating to the recognition of foreign insolvencies and office holders of foreign insolvent companies.

United States: Like the UNCITRAL Model Law [on Cross-Border Insolvency], there is foreign main and foreign nonmain recognition. Chapter 15 of Title 11 of the United States Code (Chapter 15) defines a "foreign main proceeding" as a "foreign proceeding pending in the country where the debtor has the center of its main interests." 11 U.S.C. § 1502(4). Chapter 15 defines a "foreign nonmain proceeding as a foreign proceeding, other than a foreign main proceeding, pending in a country where the debtor has an establishment." 11 U.S.C. §1502(5). The principal difference between the two types of recognition is that if a Bankruptcy Court recognizes a proceeding as a foreign main proceeding, then the automatic stay immediately springs into effect, the debtor may sell property of the debtor in the United States and can operate its business and exercise the rights of a trustee. If a Bankruptcy Court recognizes a proceeding as a foreign nonmain proceeding, then the petitioning party must specifically request additional specified relief from the Bankruptcy Court, which it has discretion to do so and must be satisfied that the relief relates to assets that, under U.S. law, should be administered in a foreign nonmain proceeding.

United Kingdom: In the United Kingdom (subject to minor variations between the countries forming the Kingdom as a whole), recognition of a validly appointed foreign insolvency office holder can be permitted. Recognition can be granted under the laws which implement the UNCITRAL Model Law [on Cross-Border Insolvency], the [European Union] Cross Border Insolvency Regulations, the Insolvency Act 1986, or the common law which predates each of the three more recent enactments. The United Kingdom recognizes an office holder of "main proceedings" and "secondary proceedings." Main proceedings are, in summary, those commenced in the sovereign state in which the entity or individual has its "center of main interests." An office holder recognized as the main proceedings practitioner will, in general, be afforded greater powers automatically than those appointed under secondary proceedings. That will include powers of investigation, asset seizure and sale, and powers to stay proceedings or bring litigation on behalf of the insolvent estate. A recognized office holder of secondary proceedings might have to apply specifically to court in the United Kingdom to take certain actions that a main proceedings office holder could take as of right once recognized.

Switzerland: Switzerland does not recognize the foreign trustees of foreign entities in bankruptcy. The foreign office holder can, however, apply before the civil judge (or the [Financial Market Supervisory Authority] in case of banks) for recognition of the foreign bankruptcy decree or any equivalent insolvency measures. There is only one type of recognition of foreign bankruptcies in Switzerland, which does not follow the UNCITRAL Model Law [on Cross-Border Insolvency]. Once the foreign bankruptcy decree is recognized, an ancillary bankruptcy, the so-called minibankruptcy, is opened in Switzerland. A Swiss liquidator is appointed to conduct the activities of the ancillary bankruptcy. The ancillary bankruptcy is strictly conducted in accordance with Swiss bankruptcy law (with some modifications provided for at Articles 170–174 of the [Swiss private international law act] (PILA); see below our answers to question (*g*)). The Federal Banking Act provides, however, for a simplified procedure of recognition of foreign banks in bankruptcy before the [Financial Market Supervisory Authority], where, as an alternative to the ancillary bankruptcy, the foreign trustee may be allowed to be remitted with the assets located in Switzerland (see below our answers to question (*d*)). On January 1, 2019, a revised law on cross-border insolvency—Chapter 11 of the Swiss Federal Code on Private International Law (CPIL)—entered into force in Switzerland. The amendments to the CPIL will facilitate the recognition of foreign bankruptcy proceedings and composition agreements. It will also foster international cooperation between the various courts and other competent authorities in such matters. The restrictive recognition requirements of the prior law, in particular the principle of reciprocity and the mandatory ancillary bankruptcy proceedings, have in the past impeded or delayed Swiss recognition of foreign insolvencies. Under the new law, these requirements are lifted—insolvency proceedings that were opened at the debtor's center of main interest abroad will now be recognized in Switzerland.

Australia: In Australia, a "foreign representative" can apply for recognition of foreign insolvency proceedings under the Cross-Border Insolvency Act 2008 (Cth), which implements the UNCITRAL Model Law [on Cross-Border Insolvency] in Australia.

A foreign representative is defined as a person or body, including one appointed on an interim basis, authorized in a foreign proceeding to administer the reorganization or the liquidation of the debtor's assets or affairs or to act as a representative of the foreign proceeding. A "foreign proceeding" is defined as a collective judicial or administrative proceeding in a foreign State, including an interim proceeding, pursuant to a law relating to insolvency, in which proceeding the assets and affairs of the debtor are subject to control or supervision by a foreign court, for the purpose of reorganization or liquidation. Pursuant to the Model Law [on Cross-Border Insolvency], foreign proceedings may be recognized as "foreign name proceedings" or "foreign nonmain proceedings." The form of recognition impacts upon the relief a court will grant upon recognition. When a court recognizes a proceeding as a "foreign main proceeding," certain relief (including stays of proceedings against the debtor and execution against the debtor's assets) follows automatically. On recognizing a proceeding as a "foreign nonmain proceeding," relief may be awarded at the court's discretion and the court must take into account whether the assets subject to the relief should be dealt with in the foreign nonmain proceeding (as opposed to a different insolvency proceeding, whether main or nonmain). In addition, section 29(2) of the Bankruptcy Act 1966 (Cth) provides that Australian courts must act in aid of the courts of "prescribed countries" that have jurisdiction in bankruptcy (that is, insolvency of an individual) and may act in aid of courts of other countries that have jurisdiction in bankruptcy. An equivalent provision with regard to companies can be found in section 581(2) of the Corporations Act 2001 (Cth). Although those provisions do not expressly contemplate recognition of foreign office holders, the remedies they provide tend to imply recognition of the foreign office holders and proceedings. For example, section 29 has been used to transfer assets to a foreign trustee in bankruptcy. The common law relating to the recognition of foreign insolvency officers is not well developed in Australia. It is possible for the appointment of a foreign insolvency practitioner to be recognized in Australia by operation of the common law of the recognition of foreign judgments, or by operation of the equitable jurisdiction of some courts, but this is very rare and (as far as we know) unheard of subsequent to the enactment of the Model Law [on Cross-Border Insolvency].

United Arab Emirates: No, although there are limited exceptions for the Dubai International Financial Centre (DIFC) area. The DIFC has a separate insolvency law from the rest of the United Arab Emirates, DIFC Law No. 3 of 2009. United Arab Emirates (non-DIFC) law is based on Arab Civil Law, a mixture of French Civil Code with Islamic principles from the Ottoman Majelle. There are no statutory provisions governing the recognition of foreign insolvencies or requiring the United Arab Emirates courts to cooperate with foreign insolvency practitioners. The DIFC law, which applies only to insolvency of companies and assets within the DIFC geographical area, is a common law–based jurisdiction.

Cayman Islands: Foreign office holders can be recognized in the Cayman Islands and have commenced and participated in proceedings before the Grand Court of the Cayman Islands (a superior court of record, the Grand Court) without difficulty on many occasions. Although the UNCITRAL Model Law [on Cross-Border Insolvency] is not applicable in the Cayman Islands, there are two avenues for recognition: (1)

common law recognition and (2) statutory recognition. The common law jurisdiction is set out in a substantial body of local case law and is similar to that of England, the case law of which is of persuasive value in the Cayman Islands due to its legal status as a British Overseas Territory. The statutory basis for recognition is by way of the International Cooperation provisions of Part XVII of the Cayman Islands' Companies Law (as revised) (the Companies Law), which provides a convenient statutory mechanism for the recognition of foreign trustee, liquidator, or other official (a foreign representative) appointed in respect of a foreign corporation or other foreign legal entity (a debtor) for the purposes of a foreign bankruptcy proceeding, including proceedings for the purpose of reorganizing or rehabilitating an insolvent debtor (a foreign bankruptcy proceeding), in the country of its incorporation or establishment. The purpose of Part XVII is to provide foreign representatives with a convenient and expeditious method of establishing their credentials and right to act on behalf of a debtor in a way that will have universal effect within the Cayman Islands, without the need to establish their right separately as against every individual counterparty.

b. What elements are required to be proven or established for a foreign office holder to successfully seek recognition in your jurisdiction?

Belgium: See response to question (*a*).

British Virgin Islands: The foreign office holder will need to establish that the proceedings in which he or she is appointed are a collective judicial or administrative proceeding in one of the designated countries, including an interim proceeding, pursuant to a law relating to insolvency, in which proceeding the property and affairs of the debtor are subject to control or supervision by a foreign court, for the purpose of reorganization, liquidation, or bankruptcy. Once that is established, in determining an application for recognition and assistance, the court shall be guided by what will best ensure the economic and expeditious administration of the foreign proceeding to the extent consistent with: (1) the just treatment of all persons claiming in the foreign proceeding; (2) the protection of persons in the [British] Virgin Islands who have claims against the debtor against prejudice and inconvenience in the processing of claims in the foreign proceeding; (3) the prevention of preferential or fraudulent dispositions of property subject to the foreign proceeding, or the proceeds of such property; (4) the need for distributions to claimants in the foreign proceedings to be substantially in accordance with the order of distributions in a [British] Virgin Islands insolvency; and (5) comity.

Hong Kong SAR, China: Application is made by letter of request in the foreign jurisdiction requesting the High Court in Hong Kong SAR, China seeking judicial assistance. The letter of request must be from a common law jurisdiction with a similar substantive insolvency law; and, the request must be for an order of a type that is available to liquidators under Hong Kong SAR, China's insolvency regime. By way of example, in the recent *African Minerals* case, English administrators were denied recognition to enforce a moratorium against disposal of assets, which was available to the administrators in England pursuant to the Insolvency Act [1986], as no equivalent statutory remedy was available in Hong Kong SAR, China.

Jersey: See response to question (*a*). In respect of an Article 49 application under the Bankruptcy (Désastre) (Jersey) Law 1990 made by the foreign court of a prescribed country, the request itself is deemed as sufficient authority for a Jersey court to exercise its jurisdiction to grant foreign recognition. When assisting a foreign court in this way, a Jersey court may have regard to any UNCITRAL model law on cross-border insolvency to the extent that it considers it appropriate to do so. Further, the Royal Court has discretion as to whether it applies Jersey law or the law of the requesting country when granting assistance. For applications made by foreign office holders to whom Article 49 does not apply, applications are made by way of a letter of request from the foreign court administering the insolvency. Typically, the applicant consults with the Viscount's Department (the enforcement officer of the Royal Court in Jersey) before an application is issued in Jersey in order to ensure that the order sought is drafted in suitable terms. To establish an application for foreign recognition, there has to be a valid connection between the debtor and the law under which the insolvency occurred.

Singapore: Recognition is at the discretion of the Singapore Courts and must be consistent with justice and public policy of Singapore, including that the interests of domestic creditors would not be prejudiced. There are otherwise no specific elements to be met.

United States: To seek recognition, the foreign office holder must file a petition for recognition under Chapter 15 with the Bankruptcy Court. The elements required to seek recognition under Chapter 15 are as follows: (1) a certified copy of the decision commencing such foreign proceeding and appointing the foreign representative; (2) a certificate from the foreign court affirming the existence of such foreign proceeding and of the appointment of the foreign representative; or (3) in the absence of evidence referred to in paragraphs (1) and (2), any other evidence acceptable to the court of the existence of such foreign proceeding and of the appointment of the foreign representative (11 U.S.C. § 1515(b)(1)–(3)). Also, "a petition for recognition shall also be accompanied by a statement identifying all foreign proceedings with respect to the debtor that are known to the foreign representative." 11 U.S.C. § 1515(c).

United Kingdom: This differs slightly depending on whether recognition is sought by a European Union, Commonwealth, or other overseas office holder. In broad summary, you must show that the office holder is validly appointed in respect of a legitimate "collective" insolvency process in the foreign jurisdiction. You must also explain whether the foreign insolvency process is a main or secondary process. You must also provide a number of certified copies (or originals) of supporting documentation to prove the authority and scope of the foreign proceedings.

Switzerland: Article 166 (PILA) lists five cumulative requirements for the recognition of foreign insolvency measures: (1) proper jurisdiction of the foreign bankruptcy authority; (2) enforceability in the state in which the decision was taken (the measure does not need to be final); (3) legal standing of the applicant; (4) absence of grounds for refusal of recognition according to article 27 PILA; and (5) reciprocity rights in the state in which the decision was taken (see our answer to question (*j*)). Grounds for refusal of recognition according to Article 27 PILA are the following: (1) the foreign bankruptcy decree is manifestly incompatible with Swiss public order (see our answer to question (*e*)) (this legal requirement is applied ex officio by the judge); (2) a party establishes that it did not receive proper notice under either the law of its domicile or that of its habitual residence, unless such party proceeded on the merits without reservation; (3) a party establishes that the decision was rendered in violation of fundamental principles pertaining to the Swiss conception of procedural law, including the fact that said party did not have an opportunity to present its defense (see below our answer to question (*e*)); (4) a party establishes that a dispute between the same parties and with respect to the same subject matter is the subject of pending proceedings in Switzerland or has already been decided there, or that such dispute has previously been decided in a third state, provided that the latter decision fulfills the prerequisites for its recognition. A foreign decision may not be reviewed on the merits.

Australia: *Pursuant to the [UNCITRAL] Model Law [on Cross-Border Insolvency]*: In order to obtain recognition of a foreign proceeding, the foreign representative must prove that he satisfies the definition of "foreign representative" in the Model Law. That is, he must be authorized in a foreign proceeding to administer the reorganization or the liquidation of the debtor's assets or affairs, or to act as a representative of the foreign proceeding. Article 15 of the Model Law requires the foreign representative to adduce at the time of application: (1) a certified copy of the decision commencing the foreign proceeding and appointing a foreign representative; (2) a certificate from the foreign court affirming the existence of the foreign proceeding and of the appointment of the foreign representative; or (3) in the absence of evidence of (1) and (2), any other evidence acceptable to the court of the existence of the foreign proceeding and of the appointment of the foreign representative. This Article has not been the subject of jurisprudence in Australia, and as yet there is no guidance from Australian courts as to what other evidence of the foreign proceeding will be acceptable. The foreign representative will also need to establish that the foreign proceeding is either a foreign main proceeding or a foreign nonmain proceeding. In order for a proceeding to be characterized as a foreign main proceeding, the foreign representative will need to prove that the proceeding is taking place in the jurisdiction where the debtor has the "center of its main interests." Article 16 of the Model Law provides that absent evidence to the contrary, the debtor's registered office, or habitual residence in the case of an individual, is presumed to be the center of the debtor's main interests. In order to establish that a proceeding is a foreign nonmain proceeding, the foreign representative will need to prove that the proceeding is taking place in a State where the debtor has an "establishment," which means "a place of operations where the debtor carries out non-transitory economic activity."

Pursuant to the Bankruptcy Act and the Corporations Act: Assistance under the Bankruptcy Act and the Corporations Act must be sought by letter of request from a foreign court that the Australian court act in aid of an external administration. Under the statutes, there is nothing further that is required. However, the precise form of the assistance to be provided by the Australian court would likely depend on the evidence before the court.

United Arab Emirates: A foreign office holder cannot successfully seek recognition in the United Arab Emirates courts. The authorities (non–Dubai International Financial Centre) will accept control of a foreign entity through a power of attorney if issued before a notary in accordance with the corporate law of such country.

Cayman Islands: Under the common law rules applicable in the Cayman Islands, a representative of a company, appointed by a court in its country of incorporation (that is, someone equivalent to an official liquidator or trustee in bankruptcy), is entitled to recognition automatically, without special formalities. The procedure for recognition under Part XVII is set out in the Cayman Islands' Foreign Bankruptcy (International Cooperation) Rules 2008, pursuant to which an application for recognition must be supported by evidence of, inter alia, an affidavit of foreign law that explains the powers and duties of the foreign representative under the law of the place of his appointment.

    c. **In some jurisdictions there are special rules governing the recognition of insolvency office holders of foreign financial institutions or insurance companies (such as under the Financial Markets Supervisory Authority in Switzerland). Do you have any such special rules in your jurisdiction? If so, what is required to obtain recognition?**

Belgium: No.

British Virgin Islands: No.

Hong Kong SAR, China: No.

Jersey: No.

Singapore: No.

United States: To qualify under Chapter 15, you must meet certain requirements. Chapter 15 does not apply to entities identified as being excluded from seeking relief under the Bankruptcy Code in section 109(b), which excludes, inter alia, foreign banks and insurance companies.

United Kingdom: There are special rules in the United Kingdom relating to insolvency proceedings concerning insurance undertakings, credit institutions, holding investment undertakings, or collective investment undertakings. These apply especially within the European Union. However, those rules relate more significantly toward the conduct of an insolvency proceeding involving a relevant entity, to ensure that a single set of proceedings will govern the winding up within the European Union, rather than the process of obtaining recognition per se. This is a complex area outside the scope of this high-level summary.

Switzerland: In respect of foreign banks in bankruptcy, the ordinary requirements for recognition described above at question (*c*) apply. Instead of the civil judge, however, the Swiss Financial Markets Supervisory Authority (FINMA) is competent to recognize foreign banks in bankruptcy. With the entry into force of Article 37g [of the Banking Act] on January 1, 2011, FINMA is now allowed to recognize not only foreign insolvency measures but also trustees appointed abroad. Instead of the opening of a Swiss ancillary bankruptcy, the foreign trustee is allowed to be directly remitted with the assets of the bank in bankruptcy that is located in Switzerland, when two additional requirements are met: (1) equal treatment in the foreign proceedings of bankruptcy of secured claims and privileged claims pursuant to the Swiss Federal Act on Debt Collection and Bankruptcy of the creditors domiciled in Switzerland; and (2) the other Swiss creditors are duly taken into account in the foreign proceedings of bankruptcy. FINMA will particularly pay attention to the possibility that the State where the foreign bankruptcy is open gives a particular privilege to the claims held by the State (such as taxes, justice costs), which could jeopardize the recovery of the privileged and secured claims of the Swiss creditors.

Australia: Regulation 9 of the Cross-Border Insolvency Regulations 2008 (Cth) provides that the UNCITRAL Model Law [on Cross-Border Insolvency] does not apply to certain banks under the Banking Act 1959 (Cth), general insurance businesses under the Insurance Act 1975 (Cth), or life insurance companies under the Life Insurance Act 1995 (Cth). The result of this is that there is no way for insolvency office holders of those institutions to be recognized under Australia's cross-border insolvency laws. However, those entities would be covered by Australia's domestic insolvency laws.

United Arab Emirates: No.

Cayman Islands: There are no special rules to differentiate insolvency office holders in this way.

d. **Will the court (or other relevant adjudicating body) charged with considering applications for recognition in your country likely refuse such an application if the foreign office holder was appointed ex parte or in a way which is incompatible with principles of natural justice or of procedural fairness?**

Belgium: Yes. Due process rules must have been complied with.

British Virgin Islands: As the court is exercising a discretion in deciding what, if any, assistance to provide to the foreign court through its officer, such matters will likely be taken into account in the exercise of the court's discretion.

Hong Kong SAR, China: As the application is made by Letter of Request, it would be presumed valid. If the order is obviously made in breach of principles of natural justice, it is likely that this would be taken into consideration in deciding whether the order should be granted. The fact an appointment was made ex parte would not affect its validity.

Jersey: Yes. Public policy exceptions are not codified in Jersey law but in applying its discretion when considering an application for foreign recognition under Article 49 or common (customary) law, the Jersey courts are likely to take into account principles of procedural fairness and natural justice. The UNCITRAL Model Law on Cross-Border Insolvency, which the Jersey courts may consider when dealing with an Article 49 application for recognition, provides for a "public policy" exception. It states that "the receiving court retains the ability to refuse to take any action covered by the Model Law . . . if to take that action would be 'manifestly contrary' to the public policy of the State in which the receiving court is situated."

Singapore: The Singapore Courts will take into consideration the fact that the order appointing the foreign office holder was obtained in breach of natural justice or procedural fairness, and be less inclined to recognize that foreign office holder. The mere fact that an appointment was made ex parte should not in and of itself be a material factor against recognition.

United States: Bankruptcy courts can inquire as to procedural fairness and consider principles of natural justice in granting or denying recognition. Section 1506 [of the Bankruptcy Code] provides that "[n]othing in this chapter prevents the court from refusing to take an action governed by this chapter if the action would be manifestly contrary to the public policy of the United States." 11 U.S.C. § 1506. A Chapter 15 petition recognizing office holders cannot proceed ex parte, but there is no per se rule preventing recognition of foreign office holders that were appointed ex parte.

United Kingdom: The court would not necessarily refuse an application solely because the appointment was made ex parte. However, it would be likely to do so if it found that there has been a material breach of procedure or a failure to give full and frank disclosure of all relevant facts. There are also rules that oblige the office-holder seeking recognition to explain what the effect of recognition would be in the United Kingdom on any third parties as part of their application. This is mainly aimed at avoiding "unfairness" if, for example, recognition would result in an automatic stay of on-going proceedings that could affect a third party.

Switzerland: Switzerland will not recognize foreign decisions which are rendered ex parte since this does not comply with article 27 of PILA. However, this has to be established by any concerned party and the judge will not refuse to recognize the foreign bankruptcy decree for this particular reason ex officio. Among the grounds for denial of recognition of a foreign bankruptcy decree is its manifest incompatibility with Swiss material public policy. This exception is rarely applied. In bankruptcy matters, a violation of Swiss public policy will be realized, for instance: (1) when the foreign decision on bankruptcy has a confiscatory or discriminatory nature; (2) when a creditor applies for recognition only to try to locate assets of a common debtor in Switzerland for reasons unrelated to the bankruptcy; or (3) when the nature of the claim which led to the bankruptcy violates the Swiss conception of public policy. This will be typically the case for punitive damages.

Australia: *Pursuant to the [UNCITRAL] Model Law [on Cross-Border Insolvency]:* On its face, if a "foreign representative" can show that he was appointed by the foreign court to manage the insolvency, the Model Law does not permit the exercise of any discretion by an Australian court to refuse recognition on grounds that the office holder was appointed in a way that was incompatible with principles of natural justice or procedural fairness. However, Article 6 of the Model Law provides that a court may refuse to take any action under the Model Law if the action would be manifestly contrary to the public policy of Australia. Depending on the gravity of the circumstances, it may well be found that the recognition of a foreign representative who was appointed contrary to the principles of natural justice and procedural fairness would be contrary to public policy. In addition, the court retains considerable discretion in the relief that may be awarded upon recognition. The court must be satisfied, in granting relief, that the interests of Australian creditors are adequately protected. In our view, if a court were satisfied that a foreign representative had been appointed other than in accordance with principles of natural justice and procedural fairness, it would most likely exercise its discretion to refuse substantive relief to facilitate the foreign proceeding and in that way, stymie the effect of the recognition.

Pursuant to the Bankruptcy Act and Corporations Act: Under section 29(2) of the Bankruptcy Act and section 581(2) of the Corporations Act, an Australian Court must assist the court of a "prescribed country." The prescribed countries are the United Kingdom, New Zealand, Jersey, Singapore, Switzerland, Malaysia, Papua New Guinea, and the United States (and their colonies, overseas territories, or protectorates), although the Australian court retains the discretion as to what assistance it should provide. The Australian court may exercise only such powers with respect to the matter as it could exercise if the matter had arisen within its own jurisdiction. For countries other than "prescribed countries," the Australian court retains discretion as to whether it should assist. The fact that a foreign office holder had been appointed contrary to the principles of natural justice and procedural fairness would be a significant factor weighing against the exercise of discretion in favor of a request for assistance. Even if an Australian court was bound to assist, any assistance ultimately provided would be heavily constrained if the court was of the view that the foreign officer had been appointed other than in accordance with principles of natural justice or procedural fairness. The mere fact that an appointment was made ex parte is unlikely to be a material consideration weighing against recognition under the Model Law or assistance under the Bankruptcy Act and the Corporations Act.

United Arab Emirates: Not relevant.

Cayman Islands: Not relevant.

e. **Can interim office holders like provisional liquidators or interim receivers seek recognition in your jurisdiction or does an order of appointment have to be a final order at first instance?**

Belgium: The order must be final and enforceable. However, pursuant to the International Private Law Code one can obtain an exequatur for provisional measures on the basis of the foreign decision that can still be appealed.

British Virgin Islands: Recognition and assistance is open to any "foreign representative" from the designated countries. A foreign representative is defined as a person or body, including one appointed on an interim basis, authorized in a foreign proceeding to administer the reorganization or the liquidation of the debtor's property or affairs or to act as a representative of the foreign proceeding.

Hong Kong SAR, China: If the office holder has authority to represent the insolvent company in the foreign court of his appointment, and requires judicial assistance to support that liquidation, he may apply for judicial assistance through his own court to the Hong Kong SAR, China court. If there is any doubt, in appropriate circumstances (urgency, risk of dissipation), assets may similarly be preserved through injunctive relief pending the formal appointment of liquidators or receivers.

Jersey: Provisional liquidators are not a feature of Jersey insolvency law but the Royal Court is flexible and prepared to consider innovative solutions where there has been fraud or debtors have sought to conceal assets from lawful creditors.

Singapore: If the office holder has authority to represent the insolvent company in the foreign court of his appointment, the fact that such appointment is interim in nature should not, by itself, be a bar toward recognition by the Singapore courts.

United States: Yes, interim office holders can seek recognition in the United States. A "foreign representative means a person or body, including a person or body appointed on an interim basis, authorized in a foreign proceeding to administer the reorganization or the liquidation of the debtor's assets or affairs or to act as a representative of such foreign proceeding." 11 U.S.C. § 101(24).

United Kingdom: In general, an interim insolvency measure such as provisional liquidation is capable of recognition. This is not a straightforward question, though, and depends upon the basis of recognition (whether European Union, Commonwealth, or UNCITRAL). As a general rule, if the foreign insolvency proceeding is a formal, collective, process properly enacted in the country of origin, it is likely to be capable of recognition one way or another. A "receiver" may not be capable of recognition if the appointment is not a collective one for the benefit of all creditors, but instead solely for the benefit of the appointing party.

Switzerland: Yes. Foreign insolvency measures can be recognized (see above our answer to question (*c*)) in Switzerland provided that they are enforceable (and not final) and that they are not rendered ex parte. However, the foreign trustee (whether interim or not) will never replace the Swiss ancillary liquidator. Even in cases of interim measures, an ancillary bankruptcy has to be formally opened in Switzerland (and can be revoked later depending on the final measures abroad). The applicant can apply, in its application for recognition, for conservatory measures pursuant to Articles 162–165 and 170 of the [Federal Act on Debt Collection and Bankruptcy], namely for: (1) the inventory of the assets of the debtor located in Switzerland (which equals a freeze of the assets); and (2) any conservatory measures that the judge considers to be in the interest of the creditors.

Australia: Pursuant to Article 2(d) of the [UNCITRAL] Model Law [on Cross-Border Insolvency], interim office holders can seek recognition in Australia. The fact that a foreign office holder was provisional on its own would not impact the foreign court's ability to seek the assistance of an Australian court under section 29 of the Bankruptcy Act or section 581 of the Corporations Act.

United Arab Emirates: There is no concept of provisional liquidator or interim receiver in United Arab Emirates law. Any liquidator appointed in accordance with United Arab Emirates law needs to be confirmed by a final judgment of the United Arab Emirates courts (unless there is a notarized shareholders' resolution of 100 percent of the shareholders of the company in question).

Cayman Islands: The Grand Court is unlikely to recognize foreign office holders appointed on a provisional basis, unless there are compelling reasons to do so. Further, the Grand Court's recognition will only go as far as the extent to which the foreign appointing order exists—if the appointment is subsequently superseded in the foreign jurisdiction, the former appointee will no longer be recognized by the Grand Court.

f. **Can a foreign office holder get recognized on his own or does he have to seek a joint appointment with a locally licensed insolvency practitioner in your jurisdiction?**

Belgium: If recognition is necessary (see response to question (*a*)), the request must be signed by a Belgian lawyer.

British Virgin Islands: A foreign office holder does not need to be jointly appointed together with a local insolvency practitioner.

Hong Kong SAR, China: He can be recognized on his own, for purposes of carrying out his duties as an office holder. In appropriate circumstances, (such as proof of sufficient connection, and that the company carries on business in Hong Kong SAR, China) he may also apply to the court for the liquidation of the company in the Hong Kong SAR, China courts.

Jersey: There is no requirement that a foreign office holder be jointly appointed with a Jersey insolvency practitioner.

Singapore: It will be at the discretion of the Singapore Courts whether: (1) the foreign office holder may be recognized on his own; (2) he is required to be appointed jointly with a locally licensed insolvency practitioner; or (3) he must apply to appoint a locally appointed insolvency practitioner and only the latter will be recognized.

United States: A foreign office holder may get recognition on his own. "A foreign representative may commence a case under section 1504 by filing directly with the court a petition for recognition of a foreign proceeding under section 1515." 11 U.S.C. § 1509(a).

United Kingdom: The foreign office holder can be recognized on his own and then take action in his own name once recognized.

Switzerland: The foreign office holder has legal standing to apply for recognition of the foreign bankruptcy in Switzerland but cannot ask to be appointed jointly with the Swiss ancillary liquidator, which is the sole person in charge of the ancillary bankruptcy. Note, however, that the foreign bankruptcy can bring a claw-back action before Swiss courts (Article 171 PILA). The procedure concerns only the assets located in Switzerland. All the assets of the foreign bankrupt entity that are located in Switzerland will be subject to the payment of the Swiss creditors' secured and privileged claims within the meaning of Article 219 of the [Federal Act on Debt Collection and Bankruptcy]. Once the schedule of secured and privileged claims of the ancillary bankruptcy is in force, the ancillary trustee liquidates the assets of the minibankruptcy. Once the proceeds of the liquidation have been distributed to the Swiss secured and privileged creditors, any balance remaining is distributed to the foreign bankruptcy only after a formal application before the civil judge on recognition of the foreign schedule of claims by the foreign trustee or a creditor. If the draft bill that the Swiss government circulated on October 14, 2014, is adopted, it will be possible for a foreign trustee to be recognized in Switzerland and to be remitted with the assets of the bankruptcy located in Switzerland, provided that the requirements of equal treatment of the Swiss privileged and secured creditors and the taking into account of other Swiss creditors are met (see the answer to question (*d*)).

Australia: A foreign representative may seek recognition of a foreign proceeding in Australia without being jointly appointed with an Australian practitioner. As part of the discretionary relief available upon recognition, the [UNCITRAL] Model Law [on Cross-Border Insolvency] provides that the court may appoint an Australian representative. This is usually done for the sake of convenience when there are a large number of assets in Australia to be realized. Australian courts also have a general discretion to appoint a receiver to assets in appropriate cases, but there is no requirement for a local receiver to be appointed in circumstances of a foreign insolvency.

United Arab Emirates: The United Arab Emirates courts will appoint only a United Arab Emirates registered practitioner (usually a locally registered accountant also registered with the court in question) as liquidator in the jurisdiction. The Dubai International Financial Centre (DIFC) courts will accept only a DIFC "registered practitioner."

Cayman Islands: A foreign office holder can be recognized on his own, without the need for a joint appointment with a licensed Cayman Islands Insolvency Practitioner.

g. What powers can a foreign office holder exercise in your jurisdiction once he is recognized locally? In some legal systems (such as the English common law of recognition) a local court can only permit a foreign office holder to exercise powers which are no greater than what he has been given in the place of his initial appointment. Is that true of your jurisdiction?

Belgium: Pursuant to [European Union] Regulation 2015/848, the liquidator appointed by a court which has jurisdiction pursuant to Article 3(1) (main proceedings) may exercise all the powers conferred on him by the law of the State of the opening of proceedings in another Member State, as long as no other insolvency proceedings have been opened there, nor any preservation measure to the contrary has been taken there, further to a request for the opening of insolvency proceedings in that State. He may in particular remove the debtor's assets from the territory of the Member State in which they are situated. The liquidator appointed by a court which has jurisdiction pursuant to Article 3(2) (secondary [nonmain] proceedings) may, in any other Member State, claim through the courts or out of court that moveable property was removed from the territory of the State of the opening of proceedings to the territory of the other Member State after the opening of the insolvency proceedings. He may also bring any action to set aside, which is in the interests of the creditors. In exercising his powers, the liquidator must comply with the law of the Member State within the territory in which he intends to take action, in particular with regard to procedures for the realization of assets. Those powers may not include coercive measures or the right to rule on legal proceedings or disputes. Pursuant to the Belgian International Private Law Code, the powers are those granted to him by the appointment decision.

British Virgin Islands: The orders which the British Virgin Islands court can make in aid of foreign proceedings are extremely wide and include orders: (1) restraining the commencement or continuation of any proceedings, execution, or other legal process or the levying of any distress against a debtor or in relation to any of the debtor's property; (2) restraining the creation, exercise, or enforcement of any right or remedy over or against any of the debtor's property; (3) requiring any person to deliver up to the foreign representative any property of the debtor or the proceeds of such property; (4) granting such relief as it considers appropriate to facilitate, approve, or implement arrangements that will result in a coordination of a [British] Virgin Islands insolvency proceeding with a foreign insolvency proceeding in respect of a debtor; (5) appointing an interim receiver of any property of the debtor for such term and subject to such conditions as it considers appropriate; (6) authorizing the examination by the foreign representative of the debtor or of any person who could be examined in a [British] Virgin Islands insolvency proceeding in respect of a debtor; (7) staying or terminating or making any other order it considers appropriate in relation to a [British] Virgin Islands insolvency proceeding; or (8) granting such other relief as it considers appropriate. In making any of the orders set out above the British Virgin Islands court may apply the law of the [British] Virgin Islands or the law applicable in respect of the foreign proceeding. However, the mere fact that a foreign office holder is recognized by the British Virgin Islands court will not result in his or her having the general rights and powers of a domestic office holder appointed under the Insolvency Act.

Hong Kong SAR, China: All of the powers granted in his own jurisdiction, to the extent that such powers coexist in Hong Kong SAR, China.

Jersey: All of the powers granted in his own jurisdiction. Recognition will normally be limited to the extent to which the foreign office holder needs to exercise such powers in Jersey and to the extent that the powers requested are consistent with Jersey's insolvency laws. Applicants are required to consult with the Viscount's Department (the enforcement officer of the Royal Court in Jersey) before an application is issued in Jersey in order to ensure that the order sought is drafted in suitable terms; requests need to be specific. The types of powers that have been granted to foreign office holders in the past have included the right to exercise authority over assets based in Jersey following a foreign insolvency or winding up, that is, protection and recovery of assets.

Singapore: All of the powers granted in his own jurisdiction, to the extent that such powers are recognized under Singapore law.

United States: Once a foreign office holder and foreign proceeding have been recognized either as a foreign main proceeding or a foreign nonmain proceeding, different provisions of Chapter 15 of the Bankruptcy Code will be at the foreign office holder's disposal. See 11 U.S.C. §§ 1509 and 1519–1521. Those powers are not necessarily limited to the powers that are available in the foreign jurisdiction, but the Bankruptcy Court can take these issues into consideration when granting appropriate relief. The impact would be greater in a case in which only nonmain recognition has been granted. When recognition is granted as a foreign main proceeding, certain powers, listed above, come into effect automatically with only certain other relief requiring court authorization. Conversely, when recognition is granted as a foreign nonmain proceeding, the foreign representative will have to seek court approval for most activities, which allows the court greater discretion in determining what powers the foreign office holder will have.

United Kingdom: This is a complex issue. Some powers are available pursuant to the legislation under which the office holder is recognized, and dependent on whether recognition is of a main or secondary proceeding. Those powers can include investigatory powers, bringing proceedings, and execution against assets of the insolvent estate. There is, however, recent authority which suggests that in the United Kingdom (and certain Commonwealth and common law jurisdictions), the powers afforded to a foreign office holder at common law can be no greater than those that would have been available in their home jurisdiction.

Switzerland: As mentioned above (see the response to question (*a*)), Switzerland does not recognize the foreign trustees of a foreign bankruptcy but a Swiss ancillary liquidator is appointed. Therefore, the Swiss ancillary liquidator will have the powers provided for by the [Federal Act on Debt Collection and Bankruptcy]. In banking matters, the foreign trustee has the powers that the [Financial Market Supervisory Authority] granted. In practice, Article 37g [of the Banking Act] being quite new, there is no precedent where a foreign trustee was allowed to carry out broader activities on Swiss soil than the powers that the foreign decree grants to the foreign trustee. However, a Swiss judge would probably consider that he is not competent to give greater powers in Switzerland to a trustee appointed by a foreign authority.

Australia: Pursuant to the [UNCITRAL] Model Law [on Cross-Border Insolvency], the foreign representative has access to Australian courts and the authority to commence or participate in a proceeding pursuant to Australia's insolvency laws if the conditions for commencing such a proceeding are otherwise met. Otherwise, the exercise of the office holder's powers in relation to Australian assets or creditors are generally conditioned on a requirement that the interests of Australian creditors remain adequately protected. Under section 29 of the Bankruptcy Act and section 581 of the Corporations Act, the court may exercise only such powers in relation to the foreign proceeding as it would have if the matter arose in its own jurisdiction.

United Arab Emirates: None, not normally possible under United Arab Emirates law. Within the Dubai International Financial Centre (DIFC) however, cooperation with foreign jurisdictions is encouraged when a foreign company is the subject of insolvency proceedings in the jurisdiction of incorporation (the DIFC courts are allowed to assist the foreign courts in gathering and remitting amounts maintained within the DIFC pursuant to Article 82 of DIFC Law No. 3 of 2009).

Cayman Islands: A foreign office holder has direct access to the Grand Court and may commence whatever proceeding may be necessary to collect a foreign company's assets or otherwise enforce its rights in the Cayman Islands. Upon the successful application of a foreign representative made pursuant to Part XVII of the Companies Law, the Grand Court may make orders ancillary to the foreign bankruptcy proceedings for the purposes of (1) recognizing the right of a foreign representative to act in the Cayman Islands on behalf of or in the name of a debtor; (2) enjoining the commencement or staying the continuation of legal proceedings against a debtor; (3) staying the enforcement of any judgment against a debtor; (4) requiring a person in possession of information relating to the business or affairs of a debtor to be examined by and produce documents to its foreign representative; and (5) ordering the turnover to a foreign representative of any property belonging to a debtor.

h. **Oftentimes, a foreign office holder does not need to seek a formal order of recognition abroad if all he wishes to do is to gather in some information by for instance resort to a right of any person to seek a disclosure order (such as a Norwich Pharmacal/Bankers Trust order under the English common law model or 28 U.S.C. § 1782 [Discovery in Aid of Foreign Litigation] in the [U.S. District Court]). Or if he wishes to sue a defendant in a foreign jurisdiction for relief in the civil courts and in the ordinary course (e.g., to sue an account debtor to collect monies owed to the estate he administers). All he needs to show in these instances is the standing to sue in the name of the insolvent debtor for which or whom he acts as agent. Is this option of avoiding the law of recognition** altogether available to office holders in your jurisdiction where he does not need to use the special powers of an insolvency office holder, or where he does not need to set up a local ancillary estate or to seek special protections like an insolvency stay or moratorium of actions against the estate that he administers?

Belgium: As the recognition is automatic, the liquidator's appointment shall be evidenced by a certified copy of the original decision appointing him or by any other certificate issued by the court which has jurisdiction. A translation into one of the official languages in Belgium may be required. No legalization or other similar formality shall be required.

British Virgin Islands: Yes.

Hong Kong SAR, China: Yes.

Jersey: Yes.

Singapore: Yes.

United States: Under 28 U.S.C. § 1782, if there is foreign litigation pending or reasonably contemplated, then the foreign office holder may seek documentary and testimonial evidence in the United States. As to substantive claims, subject to there being appropriate jurisdiction and standing, a foreign office holder may bring actions in the United States on behalf of the insolvent debtor. Section 1509 expressly provides that the failure of a foreign representative to commence a case or to obtain recognition does not affect any right the foreign representative may have to sue in a court in the United States to collect on or recover for a claim or debt which is property of the debtor.

United Kingdom: Yes. A foreign office holder could pursue a stand-alone claim or application for relief in some circumstances without seeking formal recognition.

Switzerland: The foreign trustee will always have to make the foreign insolvency measures recognized in Switzerland and will not be entitled to obtain directly information in Swiss civil proceedings. However, the foreign trustee that is not recognized in Switzerland can lodge a criminal complaint, on behalf of the bankrupt company, before Swiss criminal authorities when, before or after the bankruptcy, cross-border criminal behavior took place (such as fraud, embezzlement, or criminal mismanagement). Under Swiss Code of Penal Procedure (CPP), an entity who has been harmed by a crime may participate in the Swiss criminal investigation into those crimes in support of the prosecution, even if it has no claim for damages against the perpetrator. This allows the foreign legal representatives of the bankrupt entity to lodge a criminal complaint and to participate in the criminal investigation, even before recognition of the foreign insolvency. The right to consult the file exists for all the parties, including the plaintiff, at the latest at the moment when the suspect has been heard for the first time and the other main evidence has been gathered (art. 101 CPP). This right may be restricted for a limited time to prevent abuses (art. 108 CPP). The use of the copies levied from the file for use in other criminal or civil proceedings, in Switzerland or abroad, is, in principle, allowed.

Australia: Yes.

United Arab Emirates: The United Arab Emirates (non–Dubai International Financial Centre [DIFC]) courts have no concept of "disclosure order." It is, however, possible for a foreign office holder to use the DIFC courts to obtain a disclosure order (*Norwich Pharmacal* or *Bankers Trust*) depending upon whether the DIFC courts have jurisdiction for such order (that is, is the defendant or asset in question within the DIFC's jurisdiction?).

Cayman Islands: See the answer to question (*g*).

i. **Does your law of recognition require any form of reciprocity to be shown in the legal system of an office holder's place of appointment? If so, what kind of reciprocity is required to be shown?**

Belgium: No

British Virgin Islands: Only to the extent that the need for reciprocity could be said to be relevant to considerations of comity.

Hong Kong SAR, China: See [various responses] above.

Jersey: The countries prescribed under the Bankruptcy (Désastre) (Jersey) Order 2006 have, through their own domestic insolvency regimes, offered reciprocal treatment to Jersey. In the case of other jurisdictions, Jersey will recognize a foreign office holder on the basis of comity. Jersey does not demand absolute reciprocity, and it is not a requirement that has been codified or for which a legal test has been articulated by the courts. Nevertheless, there have been instances where the Jersey courts have considered a note from foreign counsel which states that the requesting foreign jurisdiction would offer similar assistance if Jersey were to make a similar request.

Singapore: There is no requirement for reciprocity, but its existence will be a factor toward the exercise of the Singapore court's discretion.

United States: To qualify for recognition, a foreign office holder must satisfy the provisions of section 1515 [of the Bankruptcy Code]. That section does not have a reciprocity requirement.

United Kingdom: Not as such, but it could be a factor in an unusual case involving an unusual jurisdiction.

Switzerland: Swiss law requires that reciprocity be granted in the State where the bankruptcy decree was granted. The requirement of reciprocity is not interpreted in a strict manner. The applicant will have to show that the foreign law provides for significantly similar rules but not that the foreign law provides for strictly the same rules. Generally, legal advice on recognition of foreign bankruptcy in the State where the bankruptcy decree was rendered will suffice. Reciprocity will usually be given for decrees coming from a country that adopted a law following the UNCITRAL Model Law [on Cross-Border Insolvency].

Australia: There is no requirement for reciprocity.

United Arab Emirates: Yes, "reciprocity" is usually required but even in circumstances of "reciprocity," an office holder appointed abroad would be unlikely to be accepted by the United Arab Emirates (non–Dubai International Financial Centre) authorities unless armed with an appropriate notarized power of attorney as formal legal representative of the company in question.

Cayman Islands: No.

Notes

1. The contributors to the survey were: Emmanuel France, Field Fisher Waterhouse LLP (Belgium); Shane Donovan, Martin Kenney & Co., Solicitors (British Virgin Islands); Jeff Lane, Tanner De Witt Solicitors (Hong Kong SAR, China); Stephen Baker, Baker & Partners (Jersey); Sanjeev Ghurburrun, Geroudis (Mauritius); Danny Ong, Rajah & Tan Singapore LLP (Singapore); Edward Clarkson, Munsch Hardt Kopf & Harr (United States); Alex Jay, Gowling WLG (United Kingdom); Yves Klein and Antonia Mottironi, Monfrini Crettol & Associes (Switzerland); John Mitchell, Arnold Bloch Leibler (Australia); Richard Briggs, Hadef & Partners (United Arab Emirates); Collette Wilkins, Walkers Global (Cayman Islands); Karishma Beegoo, Appleby Global (Seychelles); Athina Chatziadamou, Andreas Neocleous & Co. LLC (Cyprus); and Kees van de Meent, Höcker Advocaten (Netherlands).
2. The survey was conducted by Martin Kenney & Co., Solicitors (British Virgin Islands), as the lead member of a consortium consisting of Aarna Law (Bangalore and New Delhi), Husch Blackwell (Kansas City, MO), and certain members of ICC Fraudnet.

Appendix B. Website Resources

International Organizations and Bodies

World Bank Group

- World Bank: http://www.worldbank.org
  - World Bank Insolvency: http://www.worldbank.org/en/topic/financialsector /brief/insolvency-and-debt-resolution
  - Financial Market Integrity Group: http://www.worldbank.org/en/topic /financialmarketintegrity
- World Bank Doing Business: http://www.doingbusiness.org/

Stolen Asset Recovery (StAR) Initiative

- StAR: http://star.worldbank.org

United Nations

- United Nations: https://www.un.org
- United Nations Office on Drugs and Crime: https://www.unodc.org
- United Nations Convention Against Corruption (UNCAC): https://www.unodc .org/unodc/en/treaties/CAC/
- United Nations Convention Against the Illicit Traffic in Narcotic Drugs and Psychotropic Substances, 1988: https://www.unodc.org/unodc/en/treaties/illicit -trafficking.html
- United Nations Convention Against Transnational Organized Crime (UNTOC): https://www.unodc.org/unodc/en/organized-crime/intro/UNTOC.html

United Nations Commission on International Trade Law

- UNCITRAL: https://uncitral.un.org/
- Working Group Documents: https://uncitral.un.org/en/working_groups
- UNCITRAL Colloquia Materials: https://uncitral.un.org/en/colloquia

Organisation for Economic Co-operation and Development Convention on Combating Bribery of Foreign Public Officials in International Business

Transactions: http://www.oecd.org/corruption/oecdantibriberyconvention.htm

Inter-American Convention against Corruption:
http://www.oas.org/en/sla/dil/inter_american_treaties_B-58_against_Corruption.asp

Council of Europe Conventions and Groups: http://conventions.coe.int

Civil Law Convention on Corruption, November 4, 1999: https://www.coe.int/en /web/conventions/

Convention on Jurisdiction and the Enforcement of Judgments in Civil and Commercial Matters (Convention of Lugano): https://curia.europa.eu/common /recdoc/convention/en/c-textes/lug.htm

GRECO Group of States Against Corruption: https://www.coe.int/in/web/greco/home

Decisions and Regulations from the Council of the European Union: https://eur-lex .europa.eu

African Union Convention on Preventing and Combating Corruption, 2003: https:// au.int/en/treaties/african-union-convention-preventing-and-combating-corruption

Financial Action Task Force (FATF) on Money Laundering: http://www.fatf-gafi.org

Organizations, Rating Agencies, and Bar Associations that Track Asset Recovery Attorneys

International Chamber of Commerce: https://www.iccwbo.org/

U4, The Anti-Corruption Resource Centre: https://www.u4.no/

FraudNet: http://www.icc-ccs.org/home/fraudnet

The World Bank International Corruption Hunters: https://www.worldbank.org/en /about/unit/integrity-vice-presidency/brief/International-Corruption-Hunters-Alliance

Chambers and Partners: https://www.chambers.com

Online Sources for Case Law

StAR Corruption Cases DataBase: https://star.worldbank.org/corruption-cases/?db=All

British and Irish Legal Information Institute (BAILII): https://www.bailii.org

French legal framework and case laws (Legifrance): https://www.legifrance.gouv.fr (English translation available)